Ghosts, Murders and Scandals
of
Worcestershire II

Ghosts, Murders and Scandals
of
Worcestershire II

Anne Bradford

BREWIN BOOKS

First published in Great Britain
by Hunt End Books 2009

This edition published by
Brewin Books Ltd, 56 Alcester Road,
Studley, Warwickshire B80 7LG in 2017
www.brewinbooks.com

ISBN: 978-1-85858-567-3

A Cataloguing in Publication Record
for this title is available from the British Library

Printed in Great Britain by
Berforts Ltd.

THE AUTHOR

Anne Bradford is a retired teacher of English and commercial subjects, with a keen interest in local history. She has written three oral history books and has co-authored a range of oral history booklets with Mike Johnson.

Her interest in curious tales began in 1991 when she discovered a collection of local ghost stories in Redditch library going back to 1850. She realised that not only are they an entertaining read, but they capture the ethos of the time in a way that the history books rarely achieve. This is her twelfth collection of ghost stories, one was co-authored with David Taylor and another three co-authored with the late Barrie Roberts.

Anne is married to a graphic designer who also writes books, and has three adult children and one grandson.

THE EDITOR

This book has been edited by Denise Bonham, Principal Library Assistant at Redditch Library.

THE ARTIST

The picture on the cover is by Pamela Gregg, a part-time HNC Fine Art student at NEW College in Bromsgrove. (Her husband is a member of Parasearch).

Worcester Cathedral at night.

CONTENTS

Introduction by David Taylor, Chairman of Parasearch

An asterisk denotes not real name.

ACKNOWLEDGEMENTS

The staff of Worcestershire Record Office
and the Family History Centre.
Tim Merridew, computer expert.
George Gregg, Parapsychologist.
David Morrison at Worcester Cathedral Library for
information on Eiken Basilika and other historic details.
Rob Jarrett for props for several photographs.
Librarians at Bromsgrove, Kidderminster and Redditch.
John Bradford for help and advice.
Other acknowledgements have been listed in the text.

The motif on the corner of the pages is from a 19th century drawing by James Woodward of the black dog haunting the Bordesley meadows. He believed it to be the spirit of the Black Dog of Arden, the Earl of Warwick, who was buried in Bordesley Abbey in about 1313. See page 111.

Traditionally, a ghostly black dog is a harbinger of death.

More details are in the Bordesley Abbey Visitor's centre.

DAVID TAYLOR

The introduction is by David Taylor, a well-known and respected researcher of the paranormal.

He is Chairman of Parasearch, which he founded in 1986 to investigate paranormal phenomena in the Midlands. He is an investigator and former executive committee member of the Association for Scientific Study of Anomalous Phenomena (ASSAP), committee member of the Unitarian Society for Psychical Studies and a member of the Society for Psychical Research, the Ghost Club and the Churches Fellowship for Psychical & Spiritual Studies. Along with members of Parasearch he has spent countless nights in a variety of alleged haunted locations around the country. David has appeared on television and radio relating to the paranormal and has lectured to a variety of organisations including the National Trust, The Architecture Centre and various national charities on many aspects of parapsychology, folklore and history. He has co-authored one book (with Anne Bradford) of ghost stories and has had his research published in magazines including 'Fortean Times' and 'Paranormal' magazine. David is a professional graphic designer who runs Parasearch with his wife, Carolyn.

On the rare occasions when he is not investigating the paranormal, he can be found either in the company of his cat Felicity, or in old churches or second hand bookshops.

INTRODUCTION

*It is wonderful that five thousand years have
now elapsed since the creation of the world and
still it is undecided whether or not there has
ever been an instance of the spirit of any person
appearing after death. All argument is against it;
but all belief is for it.*

Samuel Johnson

Most of us have at some time been asked, or have asked the question
"do you believe in ghosts?" On the face of it, this is a strange question
in view of the fact that ghosts, apparitions and poltergeists have been
reported all over the world for thousands of years, often by people
who's word we would accept without question on any other matter.

Perhaps the question is best put another way "do you accept that
people have experienced encounters with what they believe to be
ghosts?" Even the most hardened rationalist would have difficulty in
saying "no!" The distinction is important because it leaves open the
controversial issue of whether there are ghosts 'out there' occupying
space or whether they are hallucinations.

The rationalist will argue, from a sceptical position, that such things as
ghosts are impossible. But, to be of value, scepticism must be informed.
Psychical research has been challenged by many sceptics during it's long
history, but few of them have taken the trouble to make a proper study
of the evidence. Most have argued from a priori position – it can't be, so
it isn't – so their comments are valueless. To be of value, scepticism must
be constructive. It is not enough for the sceptic to indicate the shortcom-
ings of an explanation; they must be able to offer a better one.

For as long as men and women have buried their dead, they have
imagined their return. But what is a ghost? How do we define what we
mean by the term 'ghost'? Historically, the word can be traced back to
Indo-European 'ghois' or 'gheis', which also produced the Old Norse
word 'geisa' meaning rage, and the Gothic word 'usgaisjan' meaning
terrify. The Old English form of the word was 'gast', which in Middle
English became 'gost'. The 'gh' spelling was probably inspired by the
Flemish 'gheest' and first appeared at the end of the 15th century. In
the Middle Ages, the word ghost was simply a synonym for 'spirit' or
'soul'. It did not acquire it's modern connotations of the 'disembodied
spirit of a dead person appearing to the living' until the 14th century.

But what do we mean when we say ghost? Many great minds in psychical research have grappled with this tricky definition, but perhaps the best description is used by the parapsychologist Michael Thalbourne: 'A sensory experience in which there appears to be present a person or animal (deceased or living) who is in fact out of sensory range of the experient'. (Thalbourne, 1982)

For those who believe that ghosts are purely the spirits of the dead, the categorisation of ghosts and apparitions undertaken by G.N.M Tyrrell in the 1940's is certainly food for thought. Tyrell was an electrical engineer who had worked with Marconi and was an influential psychical researcher. He divided reports of apparitions into four separate categories; experimental apparitions, crisis apparitions, post-mortem apparitions and finally ghosts. The first category (experimental) refers to cases where a living person attempts to project an apparition of themselves to another living person. The second category (crisis) concerns people who are undergoing a crisis of some kind, such as a life threatening illness or accident, who appear to the living at the time of the crisis. Tyrell's third category is the post-mortem apparition, and this involves the likeness of a person who is known to have been dead for at least twelve hours appearing to a living witness. The final category is the ghost. For Tyrell, there was an important difference between post-mortem apparitions and ghosts. Ghosts appear to haunt a specific location, indeed to be place centred, and to be less aware of their surroundings (Tyrell, 1973).

As we have seen with Tyrell's first category, sightings of ghosts are not always of the dead. In the 1880's the Society for Psychical Research carried out a large scale study of ghosts and apparitions. Members of the public were asked 'Have you ever, when believing yourself to be completely awake, had a vivid impression of seeing, or being touched by a living or inanimate object, or of hearing a voice, which impression, so far as you could discover, was not due to any external physical cause?'. The 17,000 replies the Society received showed that about one person in ten answered 'yes'. Of all of the results received, the majority of apparitions reported were apparitions of the living (Gurney, Myers, Podmore, 1886). Apparitions of the living are also known as doppelgangers, or by the more technical sounding, autophany (Green and McCreery, 1975).

Ghosts have a history that goes back at least as far as classical Greece; indeed the oldest known ghost story appears in the Sumerian 'Epic of Gilgamesh' written around 2000 BCE. Most of the dead in ancient Greece, such as those who died under 'natural' circumstances and had the appropriate funeral ceremonies performed, passed peacefully into the realms of

Hades. But some of the dead (such as those who died untimely or violent deaths) remained trapped between the two worlds (Felton, 1999).

The respected historian Keith Thomas has this to say about historical accounts of ghosts, "In medieval England it was fully accepted that dead men might sometimes return to haunt the living" (Thomas, 1971). He notes that the Catholic church of the time rationalised this belief by regarding such apparitions as the souls of those trapped in Purgatory. On the other hand, early Protestant preachers regarded ghosts as either popish fraud or demons. To ask someone in the sixteenth century whether or not they believed in ghosts was akin to asking if they believed in transubstantiation or the papal supremacy. Such things were just taken for granted.

An interesting question seldom asked by many people interested in ghosts, is why do tales of pre-Reformation monks, sixteenth century Elizabethans and seventeenth century Civil War ghosts predominate over those from later eras? More crucially, why do people only start seeing ghosts of people from earlier periods after about 1680? Indeed such sightings are rare until the late nineteenth century. The folklorist Jeremy Harte makes this poigniant observation, "nobody saw the ghosts of Roman soldiers in Dorset until the arrival of mass education taught the public that there had been such things as Roman soldiers and then they started popping up all over the place" (Harte, 2001).

The most popular explanation for a ghost is the 'spirit hypothesis'. In its simplest form, it suggests that a ghost is the spirit or soul of a person that survives bodily death. There are a variety of explanations as to why the spirit of a person should return after death; an attachment to the location or a person they are haunting, a call for assistance (perhaps to help the 'spirit' deal with unfinished business) or the intent on behalf of the ghost to offer comfort to a loved one.

An alternative paranormal explanation to this is the 'super-ESP hypothesis', which suggests that ghosts are not the spirits of the dead, but are the result of a telepathic communication from a living or dying person to the witness. Memories about the deceased person are projected by ESP (extra-sensory perception) from those who knew them to the person who is having the apparitional experience. This was a popular theory among the victorian Cambridge academics such as Frederick Myers and Edmund Gurney who founded the Society for Psychical Research in 1882. In recent years it has become less popular.

Another theory is that ghosts are the 'recordings' of past events, somehow recorded onto the fabric of a building or local environment. This has become known as the 'Stone Tape Theory' after the 1970's

TV drama 'The Stone Tape' by Nigel Kneale. Like many theories for ghosts and apparitions, this theory is much older than its 1970's namesake. The theory became popular through the support of the victorian scientist Sir Oliver Lodge, Professor of Physics and Mathematics at Liverpool University and Principal of Birmingham University. Lodge suggested that grief and suffering are recorded onto the 'ether' at the place where these emotions occurred, and are somehow 'played back' at a later date. (Lodge, 1929)

There are many other ways of accounting for ghostly experiences which are more mundane and which do not require notions of 'other worlds' and the supernatural. The most popular of these theories suggests that ghosts are hallucinations originating from the mind of the witness. The Diagnostic and Statistical Manual of Mental Disorders IV defines hallucinations as 'a sensory perception that has the compelling sense of reality of a true perception but that occurs without external stimulation of the relevant sensory organ'. The DSM IV also notes that it is possible to have transient hallucinations without having a mental disorder. In 1960 for example, Dewi Rees, a medical doctor practising in Wales, began a study of the effects of bereavement on widows. His research showed that 46.7% of widows surveyed had an experience of the dead spouse that they considered to be significant and real. Rees discovered that men and women reported their experiences in roughly equal numbers. Social isolation was not a factor in determining the frequency of these experiences; neither were the religious backgrounds of those questioned. Rees concluded that the sense of presence of a deceased spouse was "a perfectly normal occurrence and compatible with a favourable outcome to the process of mourning" (Rees, 2001).

An important factor when examining reports of ghosts is the psychology of the witness. There is good evidence that people can have ghostly experiences simply by suggestion. Psychologists James Houran and Rense Lange tested this idea by taking 22 participants individually around five different areas of a dilapidated theatre. Half of the participants were told that the research was concerned with investigating paranormal activity in the theatre while the other eleven were told that the premises were under renovation and the research was examining people's reactions to such environments. Participants were asked to report any experiences they may have while in the theatre. The results showed that those from the 'paranormal' group reported significantly more strange experiences than the 'renovation' group (Houran and Lange, 2001) .

One of the most frightening of ghostly experiences is termed the 'Old

Hag' experience. It occurs at night, and involves people who are asleep being woken up by the sensation that either a strange presence is in the room with them or that an 'Old Hag' is sitting on their chest. People who report having this experience also report that they are unable to move during the terrifying encounter (Hufford, 1982). As strange as this experience may sound, it has a rational explanation – the known medical condition called sleep paralysis.

Closely associated with reports of ghosts and hauntings are poltergeists. The word is German in origin and means 'noisy spirit'. Poltergeists are often associated with disruptive outbursts such as objects being thrown, water appearing out of nowhere and fires starting. One of the earliest documented reports of poltergeist activity comes from the 12th century Archdeacon of Brecon, Giraldus Cambrensis. He wrote of his journey through Wales, and how he encountered two noisy and mischievous spirits (Cambrensis, 1944).

There are three main theories for poltergeists. The first and most popular theory is that they are 'spirits of the dead'. This theory gained some unusual support from the psychiatrist Ian Stevenson who suggested that spirits of the dead may be responsible for more cases than people realise (Stevenson, 1972). The second theory sees them as originating from the human mind. The ability of the human mind to influence and move physical objects is called psychokenisis – mind over matter. Respected psychical researcher Dr.William Roll examined 116 poltergeist cases spanning 400 years in more than 100 countries. His research led him to come up with an exciting new theory – Recurrent Spontaneous Psychokenisis – (RSPK). A similar theory was suggested in the 1930's by the psychiatrist Nandor Fodor, who favoured a human origin for poltergeists. Finally, there is the electromagnetic theory. Canadian scientist John Huchison discovered, by accident, that electromagnetic equipment in his laboratory, when turned on, made objects move, pools of water appear and even metal objects bend and levitate (Budden, 1996). Like a lot of things in psychical research, this was nothing new! Again, researcher William Roll investigated 12 sites where a variety of paranormal phenomena had been reported. When he investigated these sites he measured electromagnetic fields (EMF), geomagnetic fields (GMF) and ion densities. Roll was not alone in thinking there was a link between hauntings and EMF and GMF. Canadian scientist Dr. Michael Persinger has also suggested that exposure to bursts of these fields may result in people believing they have seen ghosts. Persinger has done more research than anyone else in laboratory conditions to show that when the human brain is exposed to these transient fields, people believe they have had a paranormal experience. (Persinger, M.A. & Koren, S.A. 2001) To return to Roll's research, his investigations showed that of the 12 locations investigated, three showed significant EMF activity, six sites showed GMF higher than the norm and high positive ions readings were found in seven locations. These findings tentatively suggest that increased EMF and GMF combined with the mood altering properties of increased positive ion densities might lead to people seeing ghosts. As with all theories for the paranormal, a good deal more research still needs to be done to convince everyone (Braithwaite, 2008). The final theory to have become popular in recent years involves infrasound. The human ear is able to distinguish sounds between 16Hz and 20kHz, anything below this cannot consciously be heard by humans. In 1998 Vic Tandy, a researcher from Coventry University had a strange experience while working late in his workshop. He felt that some invisible presence was in the room with him. When he returned to the workshop the next day to repair his fencing foil, he noticed that when placed on his workbench the blade began to vibrate. By diligent research he was able to show that the vibration was caused by low frequency sound (infrasound) in the region of 19Hz caused by a nearby industrial fan (Tandy and Lawrence, 1998). Further research has shown that infrasound has been linked to causing people to believe that invisible presences are in the same room and can even make some people believe they have seen 'figures' out of the corner of their eye (Tandy 2000). Research by Tandy (who sadly died a few years later) and others may indicate that infrasound could be responsible for a small proportion of ghostly experiences, although some researchers remain sceptical (Braithwaite and Townsend, 2006).

As you settle yourself down to read the stories in this book, remember that ghosts are a complex phenomenon, worthy of your serious attention. If you are looking for an explanation to the stories you read in these pages, perhaps you would be wise to remember the words of author and researcher Paul Devereux, "It might therefore be best for us to not totally disbelieve in the reality of spirits and yet not automatically assume that they are simply the ghosts of the dead or beings from the Otherworld either. They may be part of a reality for which our culture does not yet have working concepts" (Devereux, 2001).

David Taylor
Chair, Parasearch, www.Parasearch.org.uk

A list of David's references can be found at the end of the book.

1. THE WORCESTER AREA

n the heart of Worcester, the mediaeval walls of Worcester Cathedral tower over the river Severn. A cathedral has stood on this site for more than 1,300 years. The first building probably goes back to 680 and was rebuilt about three hundred years later, but it was badly damaged by Danish pirates in 1041 who swept down the river Severn. An old legend said that one of the Danes tried to carry away the great sanctus bell but it was too heavy for him, he lagged behind the others so that the citizens caught him. They flogged him to death and nailed a piece of his skin to the door of the cathedral to deter other raiders. The Victorians replaced the door and put the old one, complete with its skin, into storage. Recently, a part of the skin was sent off for testing and it turned out to be human skin of about the right period, so the old legend turned out to have some truth in it.

Saint Wulstan's bones

A new cathedral was built in 1084, in the time of William the Conqueror. The inspiration for the building came from Saint Wulstan who was appointed bishop of Worcester in 1062. He was the only Saxon bishop to hold his post under Norman rule and was one of the most important men in England. The church then had enormous power both politically and spiritually, and he administered the kingdom of Mercia, which included all Worcestershire, Gloucestershire and West Warwickshire. Amazingly, parts of his church have survived, mainly the awe-inspiring crypt.

Saint Wulstan lived to be 87 years old and died in 1095. He was canonised in 1203 and a beautiful golden shrine was built to hold his remains. Miracles began to occur at his shrine, Worcester became a centre of pilgrimage and fifteen or sixteen people were cured every day. Unfortunately the gold had to be extracted to pay a fine. Another fire in 1202 caused a great deal of damage but by 1218 the cathedral had been renovated and a new tomb built for Wulstan. A grand opening ceremony was arranged at which the young Henry III, five English bishops, four Welsh bishops, seventeen abbots and a large number of noblemen were present. The *Victoria County History* states:

> To the bishop (bishop Sylvester) it was an unfortunate day. A new and very gorgeous shrine had been repaired for St Wulstan (his body), since the precious metals on the old one had been melted down to pay the fine placed on the monastery for submitting to Prince Louis

and the French. There was some difficulty in getting St Wulstan to fit into his new shrine, which was not long enough for him. The bishop thought that if all the bones were placed within it, the mode in which they were placed did not very much matter; so 'with his own hand', says the chronicler, 'he cut them up, placed them in the shrine, and praised himself for the deed.' This impious act took place on 6 June; on the 16 July the bishop was dead; St Wulstan had avenged himself!

Henry VIII, King of scandals

The year 2009 marks 500 years since Henry VIII came to the throne. The scandals surrounding him are well known, how, after twenty years of marriage, he decided to divorce Catherine of Aragon and marry Anne Boleyn. The Pope refused to sanction Henry VIIIs divorce, so he dispensed with the Roman Catholic Church, and made himself head of the Church of England. The results can be seen today, in the pitiful remains of three great Worcestershire abbeys at Redditch (Bordesley), Evesham and Pershore. Other monasteries were closed. With them and their occupants went the Roman Catholic faith, education, care of the sick and elderly, travel accommodation, husbandry and a thousand other skills.

Many refused to convert from Roman Catholicism. There were repeated attempts to put a Roman Catholic on the throne, the most famous being the gunpowder plot of 5th November 1605, still remembered with fireworks and bonfires. It was led by several wealthy, well-educated young men, many from Worcestershire. They planned to blow up the Houses of Parliament, kidnap five-year old Prince Charles and govern the country in his name. The great houses in Worcestershire which became involved one way or another were Huddington Court, Hewell Grange (now a remand home), Harvington Hall, Hagley Hall, Grafton Manor, Hindlip Hall and, just over the border in Warwickshire, Coughton Court.

King John and his passions

Not so well known are the scandals surrounding King John who reigned 300 years before Henry VIII, from 1199 to 1216. John's lovesick passions cost him Normandy, the crown jewels and, according to rumour, his life! He now lies in the heart of Worcester Cathedral in a finely-carved tomb of Purbeck marble.

Born in 1167 he was the youngest of Henry II's sons and his father's favourite but despite this, he went to war against him. He also plotted against an older brother, King Richard, during his reign. A teenage nephew raised

Far left: An old woodcut of the tomb of King John where he lies between tiny effigies of Saint Oswald and Saint Wulstan. Near left: Portrait of King John.

arms against England in France and when he was captured, John ordered that he was to be blinded and castrated. This was never carried out but John finally killed his nephew in a drunken rage.

He disagreed with his barons and was forced to sign the agreement known as the Magna Carta, which he contravened many times. A quarrel with the Pope resulted in England being placed under an interdict for six years. No new churches could be built and no services could be held. No-one could get married and the dead were buried without a funeral service.

At the age of nine John was betrothed to a wealthy heiress, Isabella of Gloucester, and he married her at the age of 21. The king of England was also the king of Normandy, consequently John frequently travelled between the two countries. He became infatuated with the daughter of a French Count, also named Isabella, but unfortunately she was already betrothed elsewhere. If there was something King John wanted, nothing would stop him. He divorced the first Isabella which annoyed the English courts, especially as he kept her estates, and married the second Isabella. Her slighted suitor was so enraged that he invaded Normandy and took it from the English.

However, John had his good points. He was, for example, the only medieval king to stabilise the country. He founded Liverpool and introduced a new coin, the British penny. He had a 'caring' side, he protected the Jews, he wrote 'thank you' letters, and he took an interest in the administration of justice and travelled about, hearing and judging various cases.

King John was always very good to the monks at Worcester. He visited regularly which gave the cathedral great prestige. (He could indulge his passion for hunting in Worcestershire's great forests.) He restored confiscated land to the monks and granted various privileges such as markets and fairs both to them and to their villages. On one of his last visits he waived part of their taxes so that they could repair damage to the cathedral.

In 1216 the barons went to war against King John and turned to France for support. A French army reached London. The king marched his men across eastern England, burning and plundering as he went. He reached

Wishbech and attempted to cross the Wash. He himself got across safely but the returning tide overtook his long train of horses and baggage wagons so that he was forced to stand and watch while they sank into the quicksands. Gone was the money to pay his soldiers, together with arms and provisions, and worse still, all the crown jewels. He flew into a rage.

King John spent that night at the Abbey of Swineshead in Lincolnshire. By this time he was nearly fifty years of age and extremely fat. His rage does not seem to have affected his appetite, and he had a hearty meal of lamphreys (a kind of eel) washed down by fresh beer. He soon fell extremely ill. He was carried on the back of a horse to Newark-on-Trent where he made his will. Amazingly, Worcester Cathedral library has the original 800 year old will. A section reads, 'I desire that my body be buried in the Church (the cathedral) of St Mary and St Wulstan of Worcester'.

Three days later, in October 1216, he died. The abbot of Croxton carried out a post mortem in which John's intestines were found to be very much swollen. The abbot decided to keep his intestines, so the King was buried without them.

Fifty years later gossip began to emerge from several sources that one of the monks at Swineshead had poisoned the king's lamphreys. John had become enamoured of the abbot's sister, and the monk wished to save her honour. The incident is so well-known that three centuries later Shakespeare referred to it:

The King, I fear, is poison'd by a monk;
I left him almost speechless.

The tale is told that King John suspected that he would not be admitted through the pearly gates so he asked to be buried between Saint Oswald and Saint Wulstan to enable him to slip into heaven unnoticed. To further achieve this, he asked to be dressed in a monk's habit over his robes. The tomb was opened in 1797 (and 'Oh! What a treat for the antiquarian,' exclaimed the sexton). The skeleton was measured at 5 feet 6.5 inches (168 cms), the average height of a medieval man. The remains of the king were intact, on one side of him lay a sword, the bones of his left arm lay across his breast, and his teeth were quite perfect. His clothes were the same as those carved on his tomb except that his crown was missing and his head and shoulders were covered by a monk's cowl.

Sometime in the fifth or sixth centuries, a wizard and prophet by the name of Merlin was said to inhabit the courts of King Vortigern and Arthur. He prophesied that a king would lie between two saints, so this is thought to be a fulfilment of the prophecy. Originally King John's effigy lay between the tombs of Saint Oswald and Saint Wulstan but a few years after his death the layout was changed and now the two saints are represented by tiny statues at his shoulders.

4

Scandal in the library

The erudite confines of Worcester Cathedral library is the last place one would expect to find a scandal, but they are there.

In the library is a collection of books from the time of King John, perhaps the king himself handled them. Worcester cathedral library is said to be the second most important cathedral library in England. It contains medieval manuscripts from the Anglo-Saxon era to the present day.

In their possession is a large, elegant tome published in 1649 entitled *The Works of Charles I with his Life and Martyrdome*, otherwise known as the Eikon Basilika. This book helped to change the whole course of English history and was the centre of a scandal which had to be hastily suppressed.

The 1600s was, of course, an eventful century. It saw the beheading of Charles I, Oliver Cromwell ruling like a king until his death, then his son taking over but proving to be useless. Finally, in 1660, the son of Charles I was recalled from exile and offered the throne as Charles II. The Eikon Basilika was published a few days after Charles I was beheaded. The title page reads 'The Pourtracture of His Sacred Majestie in his Solitudes and Sufferings'. It was said to be written by Charles I and gives his thoughts during the period leading up to his death. He appears to be a dedicated, conscientious, thoughtful, and sensitive character.

People in general were horrified by the execution of Charles I and the book created a great deal of sympathy for the Royalist cause, especially as folk were suffering under the strict regime of Oliver Cromwell. It was one of the reasons why Charles II was offered the throne when it became vacant.

A nasty shock awaited Charles II after he was crowned king. Who should turn up but John Gauden, saying that he had written the book, not Charles I. Gauden was an educated cleric holding several high posts in the church and he had visited the king while he was in prison. To keep Gauden quiet, he was promptly made King's Chaplain and appointed Bishop of Exeter. However, Gauden did not believe this to be sufficient reward as the living in Exeter was a poor one, so the king appointed him as bishop of Worcester. Fortunately for King Charles, he was only in the office for a few months before he died, leaving his widow to pick up the bills for his expenses. However, she found the money to pay for a grand monument in Worcester cathedral. It graces the wall near the door to the cathedral library.

O miserable one!

Like most great historic buildings, Worcester Cathedral has a traditional ghost. One would have thought it would have been haunted by King John or perhaps the tragic Prince Arthur, Henry VIII's older brother, who died at sixteen and rests here in one of the beautiful chantries in England. However, the resident ghost is that of Thomas Morris, a local clergyman.

From the south door of the cathedral a flight of steps leads down to the gift shop. At the foot of these steps is a stone slab with the one word on it, Miserrimus. This is the grave of Thomas Morris and it is said that if you tread on this slab, you invoke his ghost.

Thomas Morris was born in about 1660, the year in which Charles II came to the throne. Morris was everything his parents could wish for, he was intelligent, handsome and popular. He entered the church and was expected to rise to a great office. He became vicar of Claines and a minor canon at the Cathedral. When Morris was about 25 years of age, Charles II (ie Charles

Stuart) died and his brother, James II, was crowned king. Unfortunately, James was so unpopular that William and Mary were invited over to England to be king and queen, and James fled to France. All those holding a responsible office were required to swear an Oath of Allegiance and Morris refused. He may have been a 'Jacobite', ie he wanted a Stuart on the throne, not a Dutch 'stadtholder'.

Consequently, although he was a priest he was never allowed to have a parish. He spent the rest of his days living quietly and comfortably in a small house near the cathedral.

Morris's instructions for his burial were precise. He asked to be buried beneath the slab with its single word and he also asked for the covering of his coffin to be carried by six girls in white, all with a white rose, the symbol of the Jacobeans. Perhaps 'O miserable one' refers not only to himself, but also to England.

The ghost has been seen many times. Albert Price saw it in the 1920s and his favourite party piece was his version of the night he saw the ghost. In 1934, a young 17-year old was courting his girlfriend beneath the ruins of Guesten Hall when:

It was a brilliant moonlit night and as I looked up I saw what I took to be an old dear looking out of window. ... I was working at a shop in Broad Street and one morning soon afterwards I decided to go to Astons, the wholesale wood yard, to get myself a bit of cheap wood.

I jumped on my bike and on the way I thought, 'I'll go and have a look and see if that old dear is till there'. When I saw the building in daylight and had a look at it from the rear, my flesh ran cold. Nobody had been up there for years. It was a straight drop to the ground and, as well, it was thickly encrusted with moss. I can describe that person even now. I had first taken it to be an old lady but on looking back, I am sure that it was a monk. He was aged about fifty and wearing a garment with a square neck. He had shoulder length hair and a fringe. I saw him so clearly I could even see one rotten tooth in his upper jaw.

In 1978 an electrician wedged in some dark and poky little nook inaccessible by the public, thought he was having his tools handed to him by his apprentice, only to discover that the lad had gone off for the loo and a cup of tea. The electrician refused to go back and another company had to finish the job!

The Lady of the Lock

Up until about the 1900s, many roads were often nothing more than dirt tracks and deeply rutted. The best method of transport was by boat and the river Severn was the highway of the West Midlands. The river joins the Worcester to Birmingham canal at Diglis, south of the town.

A Worcestershire mum has a strange story to tell about the lock:

Going back a few years now, my son, John, had a few words with his wife and stormed out of the house. They live by the canal, near to what was the old Cadbury factory. Opposite and down a bit are the locks. He was in a mood so he marched off to cool down a bit and kept on walking. It was just getting dusk as he came near to the locks and he saw a lady sitting on the one side. He thought how strange it was that a woman should be sitting there at that time of night. It was a young woman, dressed in sixties type clothes with the big hair and the short skirt. She turned towards him and disappeared. He couldn't believe his eyes. For several seconds, he just stood still. He thought, 'Where's she gone? Has she fallen in the lake?' but there wasn't a ripple. As he walked past he looked in the bushes but nobody was about. John was so frightened that he kept quiet about it and didn't tell anyone for a long time. He's a non-believer and thought people would think he was stupid.

There's a story that in the 1960s, a woman was pregnant by another man and her husband threw her out. Of course, that was a terrible thing in the sixties and she committed suicide in the lock. Whether it was her or not he doesn't know.

Saint John's - The phantom visitor

The church was built in 1165 and a large part of this early building remains. The church and parish are probably named after John the Baptist in the New Testament. The drove roads from mid Wales, used for driving cattle, converged here so that it was a flourishing community. The narrator of the next story, a charming middle-aged lady, says:

In the 1970s I was living in St John's in Worcester. As clear as day I saw a figure going up my stairs. He was wearing clothes that looked as if he had come from the 1850s or 1870s, a big trench coat and a tall hat. I thought, 'What's he doing in my house?'. I followed him into my parent's bedroom where he went behind the wardrobe and disappeared.

Unfortunately I had a disabled person with me and I couldn't stop to investigate, I had to go.

I was a sceptic before then, I don't know now.

St John's, Blakefield - The storyteller

Blakefield is now just three short roads in St John's, Blakefield Gardens, Blakefield Road and Blakefield Walk.

When my daughter was about three, we moved into a house in Blakefield, Worcester. Most nights I could hear her talking to someone, so I asked her who it was. She told me that it was Mrs W... who sat on her bed at nights. My daughter said that Mrs W... would read her a story, then she would go off and read stories to other children, then she would come back and read her another story.

This had been going on for some months when I happened to mention it to the lady next door. She told me that the name of the old lady who lived in the house before us was named Mrs W....

SPETCHLEY - The nurse's tale

The 30 acres of Spetchley Gardens and deer park to the east of the city, are regularly open to visitors. The Berkeley family have owned the estate for more than 400 years. The first member of the Berkeley family to live here was Rowland Berkeley, a wealthy cloth merchant from Worcester, and his wife Katherine. They bought the house in 1605.

Rowland's son, Robert, became a famous judge. In the 1630s, events were hotting up between the king and parliament which eventually led to civil war. Charles I was trying to raise money to improve the navy so he imposed a loan on landowners, known as 'Ship money'. An MP from Buckinghamshire,

John Hampden, refused to pay, arguing that loans were illegal and a violation of Magna Carta. Robert Berkeley sat on the case in 1637 and found in favour of Charles I. John Hampden was thrown into prison.

The civil wars ran from 1642 to 1651, when the parliamentarians were finally victorious. Robert Berkeley was imprisoned in the tower for backing the wrong side and was told he would have to stay there until he could pay a fine of £20,000. Fortunately, parliament was short of money and so they agreed that he need pay only £10,000 if he paid it immediately.

When Robert Berkeley returned home he found his fine house in ruins. The parliamentarians had used it as a garrison then the Royalists had captured it but burned it down. Robert repaired the stables and lived there with his family for the rest of his life.

The present house dates back to about 1811.

In the grounds of the Spetchley estate and overlooking the A422 is an old brick house, known as the 'Red house'. This was the dowager house, where the Lady of the Manor lived after her husband's death. Nearby, an ornamental metal bridge crosses the A422. A local housewife says:

When I was growing up I lived in Spetchley and my father told me

Spetchley bridge across the A422 Alcester to Worcester road.

about a white lady who walks across the metal bridge that crosses the road from Spetchley Gardens. She had been seen many times and was known locally as Lady Catherine.

Lady Catherine was the wife of first Rowland Berkeley. She lies with her husband in a sumptuous effigy in Spetchley Church.

A local housewife goes on to say:

My daughter-in-law is a district nurse and a down-to-earth sensible person. But one night she had an experience which frightened her so much she trembled as she told me about it.

She and a second nurse were called out to a rambling old house overlooking Spetchley Gardens. The elderly gentleman who lived there said that the house was over 600 years old. While they were putting him to bed, he told them that, when he is in bed, a little girl comes in the doorway and walks over to his bed, a man then appears, takes her hand and leads her out. The old gentleman says that the girl stares at him. They also appear in other parts of the house.

It was pitch dark when my daughter and her colleague left and, as the house is quite isolated, the two nurses had to use a torch to see their way down a long drive and past a field to get to their car. All the way back they had an uneasy feeling and they were followed by a curious rustling noise. Suddenly, the torch went out and they were left in the dark. They had put new batteries in only the night before.

My daughter was so scared she refused to go back to the house again.

Miss Wilmott's ghost

Most of the stately homes in Worcestershire have secrets, usually priest's hiding holes, but Spetchley has a unique surprise - a 30-acre Victorian garden, virtually hidden from view. It was created on the site of an older garden in the late 1800s by Rose Berkeley and her sister Ellen Wilmott, both well-known gardeners and horticulturists.

Ellen Wilmott (1858-1934) took a fancy to a plant known as Eryngium Giganteum, a type of sea holly that scatters copious seeds before it dies in

Miss Wilmott's ghost!

the winter. Ellen always carried a pocketful of these seeds and on the many occasions when she went to visit other gardens, she would surreptitiously scatter a handful. The owner of the garden would be surprised to find this type of sea holly flourishing in his garden, sometimes many years after her visit. The plant became known as 'Miss Wilmott's ghost'.

TIBBERTON - The Bridge

Although Tibberton is near junction 6 of the M5 and frequently invaded by fishermen and bargees from the Worcester to Birmingham canal, it has remained a small, rural village.

For four-and-a half years, Colin was the licensee of the Bridge Inn. Incidentally, he is now licensee of The Jockey at Baughton and will tell you this story himself if you call in.

In 2001 I went with my wife to the Bridge Inn at Tibberton (near junction 6 of the M5) as licensee. It was an old pub, built in about 1815 or 1820 and it had been extended over the years. When the canal was in its hey-day the boatmen would call in for a drink, and sometimes stop overnight on their narrow boats whilst the horses were in the adjoining stables.

The cellars were only about five feet nine inches in height as cellars were in those days, and the main beer drop was at the front of the pub, it's now been turned into a beer garden. In the main cellar I kept the spirit store, the ice machine, the beer drop and so on but in the first cellar I kept nine or ten barrels of real ale. Flowjet pumps were used to pump the ale up to the bar through several yards of plastic piping. I never liked going down the cellar, neither did the girls who worked at the Inn. When you went down it felt cold and damp and horrible, and you had the shivers for no reason. You often felt as if someone was watching you.

Everything went well except for one thing that intrigued me quite a bit. The real ales were delivered on a Thursday morning, so every Wednesday night I would go down the cellar and put all the lines straight. Then I would get up at six or seven on the Thursday morning and find that the lines were all twisted and crossed. I thought it was probably the girls going down the cellar and tripping over them or playing around.

Then one day, a friend of ours happened to go down the cellar and she was mortified. She said there was a spirit down there, that of an old landlord from the early days who had died down there. She was able to talk to him, but I couldn't see anything and it was quite weird to see her standing there, talking to space. Apparently, the spirit told her that a barrel had been dropped onto his neck and back when he was bending over and that had killed him. Everyone said it was an accident but he wanted to tell someone that it wasn't an accident, it was murder. He didn't want to leave the cellar until he had told somebody. He insisted on showing her his injuries, although she didn't want to see them. She said to him, 'What have you been doing all this time in the cellar?'. He replied, 'I just sit here and play with the lines and twist them'. When she told me what he had said, my blood ran cold.

She told him that he couldn't stop in the cellar and he agreed to leave, but he didn't want to go immediately. He said, 'I will go in three weeks'. Believe it or not, after three weeks the place was totally different. The cellar didn't feel damp and icy, just a normal cold and the lines were never twisted and crossed again.

In Tibberton is another pub with an interesting background. 'Speed the Plough' was originally named 'Old Speed the Plough' but after a group of local parishioners sat there and plotted to kill the vicar who was too demanding collecting his tithes, they were told to remove the 'God'. For more details read 'Foul Deeds & Suspicious Deaths Around Worcester'.

CROWLE – The monk

Crowle is only a mile or so south east of Tibberton off the A422. John Leland, travelling through England in the mid 1500s, describes an ancient stone coffin found at Crowle with a man's body, wrapped in lead that had crumbled to dust. He thinks it was a Dane who was buried here. The church has a great treasure, an ornamental lectern dating back to the 1200s or even earlier.

The manor house, Crowle Court, was said to have been built in the 1200s on the site of an earlier building. When the Prior of Worcester, William Moore, retired in 1536, he was given the manor of Crowle as a gift and he lived there for four years.

Crowle Court was pulled down in 1864 and the house in the next story was built in 1866, consequently it was probably built on the site of the old manor house.

I live in an old barn that goes back to 1866 and in my house I saw the hooded figure of a monk.

It was nine o'clock in the evening; I had been away for the weekend and had just come home. I was sitting, drinking a cup of tea when, out of the corner of my eye, I suddenly saw this brown figure move across the room. I thought someone had broken in. The cowl was very much forward and it was gliding, moving slowly. It moved across the room

A brown monk, courtesy Bordesley Abbey museum at Redditch.

and then just evaporated. It was as if he stopped and when he saw me he felt that he had to go.

I don't know if it's anything to do with it but one of our neighbours had died in the middle of the night.

It would be nice to think that the ghost was that of William Moore, but he was a Benedictine who wore black robes. If anyone has an explanation as to why a Benedictine Prior would wear a brown robe, perhaps they could let the publisher know.

FERNHILL HEATH – The grey lady of Oakfield House

Fernhill Heath is only about 2.5 miles (4 km) north east of Worcester A railway station was opened here in 1853 by the Oxford, Worcester and Wolverhampton branch of the Great Western Railway but it was closed under the Beeching Acts of 1965. All that remains is a footbridge over the Worcester to Birmingham line. Fernhill Heath is now little more than a dormitory hamlet on the A38.

This is where Judy saw her one and only ghost:

As you go through Fernhill Heath towards Worcester, the River School is on the right- hand side in Oakfield House, up a long winding drive. It's in a lovely house, very attractive and quaint. There's a white lodge at the bottom of the drive and an impressive Georgian entrance. It overlooks the Malvern Hills. I believe it was the home of the assistant to the Bishop of Worcester.

It's now an Independent School but round about the 1970s or 80s it was taken over by the Education Authority and used as the County Resource Centre, from where teachers could borrow various pieces of equipment that they needed. I worked there for seven years as a librarian.

The house had a massive staircase with an ornate banister. I was running up the flight of stairs, when I looked up and I saw a lady coming down the stairs. I drew to one side so that she could get past and said, 'Oh, I'm sorry'. She was wearing a massive crinoline in a boring grey, with a hooped petticoat and pinched-in waist. Her hair was light brown and was gathered in ringlets at the top of her head. Although I couldn't see her face I guessed she was youngish. She walked quite a long way along a passage, then disappeared.

I was so preoccupied I didn't really take it in. I didn't realise what I had seen until afterwards. It was so amazing. I mentioned it to my boss and he said that he had seen her as well.

It must have been thirty years ago and it has stayed with me all these years. I don't think there's any need for anyone to worry about it as I worked there for seven years and only saw it once.

CLAINES – The Old Mug House and two spine-chilling tales

At one time many churches and monasteries had their own brewery but they have now disappeared. One of the few still in existence is the Mug House at Claines. It stands next to the church of St John Baptist, and is perhaps the only pub in England on consecrated ground. The first church at Claines is said to have been built by Saint Wulstan in the 1000s, but most of the present building dates back to the 1400s and the pub was probably built at the same time.

During the 1970s the pub had such a reputation for hauntings, with phantom footsteps, doors opening and closing, gases being turned off and flying glasses that people would come out from Birmingham in the hope of witnessing a peculiar event.

A local Probus Club held its meetings in the Mug House in 2007 and one of their members told the following two stories:

I used to live in Churchdown in Gloucestershire. Just after the last war there was a group of us, all ex-servicemen - army, navy, air force - and we used to go to different houses for a game of cards after the pubs closed.

I went to play cards at a house in Badger's Cottages. The toilet was outside, about ten steps down and round the back of the house. It wasn't dark because the moon was up and there was a street light. I got out of the toilet and I heard a crunch, crunch, crunch. All of a sudden I saw this chap, Chris Green. He was the local coalman who had lived next door but he had been dead about five or six years. I watched him with his sack of coal on his back, going down the drive as if he was going to put it on the wagon at the end of the drive. It was just as if he was still alive, I saw him as clearly as I see anyone. I thought, 'It can't be, that's impossible!'. I shot in the house and told the others. They said, 'Sit down and don't make such a fuss, we have all seen him'. Of the eight people there, five of them had seen him. Somebody said, 'He didn't do you any harm when he was alive, what harm is he going to do you now he's dead?' I asked, 'Has anybody spoken to him?'. One fellow had spoken to him and the coalman went 'Oh, oh' and groaned.

I had another most peculiar experience. Again, it was not long after the war, when we used to go to various places for a drink. A few of us had got cars but mostly we went on bicycles. We went to the Andover Sports Arms in Cheltenham, you go past the reservoir up a hill and it's at the start of the A40. We all had a drink, everybody was very happy and the other chaps said to me, 'Give us a song, John', so I sang 'To be a father's boy'. When I had finished someone who happened to be in the pub said to me, 'Are you interested in music?'. I told him that I used to be in Gloucester Cathedral Choir and two of

The Old Mughouse at Claines, perhaps the only pub in England on consecrated ground.

15

my sisters and a brother were very good on the piano. He said, 'Come and meet my wife'.

There's a little cluster of four or five houses round the back of the hotel and he lived two doors away. Three of us went with him round to his house. His wife was on the piano and I had never heard such a noise, it was as if a child was banging up and down the keyboard. Her husband said, 'It's a funny thing, she'll sit there then she'll play the most beautiful piece of music by Beethoven. Wait a minute, she has to got to get in touch with him'. We laughed but he said, 'I'm quite serious. Just wait a few minutes'. She was sitting on the piano stool, she leaned against the front of the piano for a few minutes and it was as if she was praying. Then she started to play the most beautiful Beethoven you have ever heard. I can't remember the name of the pieces now but it was absolutely astounding. She was playing away, but she stopped and said, 'He said he wants a rest now'. She told us that Mr Beethoven came to her and showed her how to play. She prayed again and all of a sudden, she started playing again. It was just like somebody possessed.

I went back to my friends and told them about it and they said, 'Rubbish'. We happened to be talking about it and a girl from the Gloucester Echo overheard our conversation. She went to visit the woman and about three weeks later an article appeared in the paper about her.

THE ALCESTER AREA (WARWICKSHIRE)

 lcester is a lovely old town on the confluence of the river Arrow and the river Alne. Nearly two thousand years ago it was a Roman station, perhaps known as Alauna. It stood on the great Icknield Street, which can still be traced along parts of the A435. In the Saxon times which followed, Alcester was of great importance. It was larger than now and had a royal palace, a monastery and three parish churches. John Capgrave, writing in the early 1400s, said that the town was very wealthy and its inhabitants were 'given to luxury and viciousness'!

Hanging Well Hill

Chris Nicholson's story needs no introduction.

If you go along the road from Astwood Bank to Evesham and turn left at the Neville Arms on the road to Alcester, that's the B4090. You will reach a hill called Hanging Well Hill. Late one Christmas Eve a few years ago, at about ten o'clock, I was driving along Hanging Well Hill on my way to meet the High Bailiff of Henley at a pub in Henley. I was going at quite a speed as I was late for the pub.

We got to the big bend on the corner of Whitmore Lane. My wife, Elizabeth, was searching for something in her handbag. Suddenly, I saw what looked like a nurse in a grey cape with a hood. She stepped right out in front of me. There was no chance of my stopping, I screamed and hit the brakes. Elizabeth heard me scream and looked up to see why but she was too late to see anything.

I stopped and went back to have a look but there was no trace of anything. There wasn't a mark on the car. I'm not certain what it was but it certainly wasn't solid as I went straight through it and there was no bang. I have very good lights on my car, I have very good eyesight and I'm not the kind of person to believe in that sort of thing. If this had happened after I had been to the pub you could understand it but it happened when I was on my way to the pub.

I found it quite upsetting. You think you have had an accident.

A friend of ours is a nurse and she told us that she was working at the hospital in Worcester when a lorry driver was taken in who had had an accident at that same spot. He said that he had swerved to avoid a grey nun. The strange thing was, that this also happened on Christmas Eve but the following year.

I have often gone back there late on Christmas Eve but I haven't seen anything strange since. I have never found out what it was. And why is the hill known as Hanging Well Hill? It sounds very sinister.

The ghost, Emily

A lively writer's group met in Alcester in recent years, and the following is a true story told at the group in 2007 by Graham, a local resident.

The tale goes back a few years, when we lived in our last house (my wife, myself and three daughters). It was an rambling old early Victorian house, but always with a warm inviting atmosphere. During the years we were there, all five of us experienced happenings, which we never told the others about until one night, sitting in the kitchen, having our evening meal, one daughter started and we all followed.

One afternoon, I was the only person in the house when I distinctly felt someone touch me on the shoulder, but nobody was there. Some time later, I saw a small grey lady, of late to middle age, standing on the landing outside my daughter' s room, before she vanished.

My daughter and other people who have slept in that room, have felt someone tuck them up in bed, but not been aware of anyone there. Then my wife was working late one night, marking books and preparing end of term reports when, despite the gas fire being on, she became aware of the room going cold and someone looking over her shoulder.

Whenever anything went missing, and it often did, we always blamed EMILY, as we had come to call our friendly, but mischievous ghost. Things would vanish and then suddenly re-appear without any rhyme or reason.

That's the gist of it. However, when we first moved there, the dog spent hours looking at a particular part of the ceiling in one room. When she died and was replaced, then the next dog also spent some time looking at a spot in the same place.

The murder of Martha Morrall (from the Studley Historian of Summer 2004, by Peter Collins, who is married to a descendent of the Morrall family.).

The road from Redditch to Studley is a busy one and many motorists will have seen the Griffin Inn on the left hand side at the bottom of Green Lane, not far from the Alexandra Hospital. This was just the front part of Abel Morrall's needle factory known as 'The Towers'.

Michael Thomas Morrall, husband of Martha, was born in Green Lane Studley on the 6th of January 1818. His uncle was Abel Morrall, who

A sad end to the Griffin Inn, formerly 'The Towers'.

built and lived in The Towers. Michael owned "Crown House" and "Crown Cottage" in Redditch Road and worked for Abel. He joined the firm at an early age and eventually ran Morrall's warehouse at 7, High Street, Manchester. He spent a considerable time away from Studley and eventually bought Balmoral House in Matlock in 1858. He was the author, in 1862, of a one-penny book on the history of needlemaking.

In Matlock, the night of the 26th of March 1891 was bitterly cold and snow was to fall the next day. At 9.30 pm, two neighbours heard an explosion, they thought it was the work of poachers. At about 10.30pm, Michael Morrall walked into the Rockside Hydropathic Establishment, some hundred yards away. He was excited and seemed in a great hurry. He asked Rowlett, the "boots", to go with him to Balmoral House as there had been an explosion and his wife, Martha, was dead. Rowlett said he would follow him back and Michael said he was going to tell his friend, Mr Jesse Davies at the Poplar Hydro. Rowlett asked two young stablemen to go with him.

On arriving at Balmoral House they could see a light through the kitchen window. After a few minutes they saw Michael Morrall coming towards them. They followed him through the parlour and into the kitchen, where Martha Morrall was sitting in an armchair by a table in front of the fire. Her right side faced the window and there was a large wound on this side of her head. Blood had run down the left hand side of her face and dropped on to the floor and also on a copy of the *Manchester Evening*

19

News of that day. A pair of spectacles, in their case, lay in the blood. Michael said "there has been an explosion but I can't find where it's come from". He looked into the fire and under the grate and in the boiler, which was full of water. Rowlett then asked how he had found her.

He said, "I went to bed at nine; I heard an explosion, called her name and then came downstairs to find her dead". Rowlett noticed the blind was pulled up five to six inches from the top and was burnt or scorched on one side. The stableman, Bradshaw noticed a broken vase on the windowsill and that a lower pane of glass was broken. Sgt. Ramshall, who arrived half an hour later, having heard that there had been a murder, established that she had been shot through the window, by someone using a gun that sprayed shot into several pieces of furniture.

Police officers gathered quickly as they thought there might be a chase and two officers were placed in charge of Michael Morrall. Superintendent Lytle arrived at 2.00pm and at once ordered that no one should see or speak to Michael. The police termed it "under surveillance for his own protection".

Over the next few days, Michael was seen to be very calm and collected and was certainly under suspicion but was not arrested. The house and grounds were meticulously searched but no gun or clues were found, although a sum of £93 (a legacy) was found in Martha's drawer. Hundreds of people gathered in the road watching the search and talking about the murder. After a few days, Michael was seen wandering around the grounds and chatting to the police. He was still their only suspect at this time.

He was a tall man, 6ft (1.82m) and naturally clever, but with little education. He was a kind man, although very eccentric. Unlike the Morralls who were mostly Catholics, he and Martha were Quakers. Michael would dress in a pepper-and-salt suit and a Quaker's billycock hat, with his long, white hair flowing over his collar. He was known locally as "rest and be thankful" because of all the seats he provided around the town. The Morralls could not keep servants because of his peculiarities, he suffered regular illness of a nervous nature, for which he spent two occasions in asylums to recover. It was rumoured that he was a womanizer. He liked attention and would regularly go and stay in one of the local Hydro's. His friends maintained that he didn't possess, nor had ever been seen to handle, a gun.

Martha was buried on Monday the 30th March, with snow falling during the interment. Michael didn't attend the funeral as relatives felt it might bring on his affliction. Various relatives looked after him during all the investigations, but a housekeeper was engaged as Miss Ellen Morrall, his niece from Studley had to relinquish her duties through illness and return home. The newspapers were drawing statements from anybody who was willing to talk to them and all sorts of theories were being put forward. Michael was suffering from extreme weakness and showing the strain of the last few weeks. He read all the newspaper reports and maintained that eventually the truth would come out. The police, however, were no nearer solving the crime, despite false clues and two people admitting to the murder, who later were to be proved liars.

On the 28th October, Joseph Rowlett from the Rockside Hydro, found Michael some hundred yards from his house, lying unconscious on the path. He called Smith from the Hydro and they carried him to Balmoral House and laid him in the parlour where Martha's remains had been placed several months before. The doctor was called, who instructed a bath man from the local Hydro to apply hydropathic treatments, although he didn't feel there was any hope of recovery. Staying at the house with the housekeeper was his brother, Edwin, a shoemaker from Redditch Road, Studley who had been there a fortnight.

Michael died at 1020am on the 30th October 1891 and was buried at St Giles church Matlock next to his wife Martha. In his will he left his "Crown House" to his brother Edwin and "Crown Cottage" to the children of his youngest brother James.

Did he murder his wife? Did he pay somebody to murder his wife? What was his motive? What was the murderer's motive? Twelve years later, on the 19th January 1904, an article appeared in *the Daily Express*, which said that, a prisoner who had died in Manchester had made the following confession - "I shot Mrs. Morrall at Matlock and it has brought me to this my death. I did it for money". No name or further details were released. Did Michael really murder Martha? At this distance of time, we shall never know.

RAGLEY HALL - The white lady of the Springs

Ragley Hall is a magnificent Palladian house built in 1688 by Robert Hooke, a contemporary of Christopher Wren. For over three hundred years the house has been owned by the Seymour family, who counted among their ranks Lady Jane Seymour, Henry VIIIs third wife. Halfway between the entrance and exit gates is a little spring, a stile and a horse trough, known as 'The Springs'.

The Marquise very kindly supplied the following for *Haunted*, published in 1992:

About a hundred years ago, a little old lady used to stand by the spring asking for a lift from any passing vehicle to Dunnington cross roads, about two miles away. When the driver turned round to assist

The white lady of the springs, an imaginary reconstruction.

the old lady out of the carriage, she would be nowhere to be seen. This became such a nuisance that complaints were made and somebody dug round the spring and found the bones of a little old lady. They were laid to rest in the in Arrow Churchyard.

However, this wasn't the end of the Lady of the Springs. Speak to the locals and they will tell you many stories of friends or relatives who have seen a white lady here. The latest anecdotes come from Jane in Abbots Salford.

My father saw a white lady at Ragley Hall. Before the war, when he was about nineteen, he and his brother Cyril would cycle to Alcester for a drink. On the way home one night he saw the white lady. He said that she came across the fields and went through the hedge towards the lake. They both cycled hell for leather home.

Two years ago my auntie was driving past that spot in a car with her husband and she saw it. I would never go that way home late at night.

3. THE ALVECHURCH AREA

y the time of the Domesday book in 1087 a church had been in existence here for many years. It has been re-built a number of times and most of the present church, except for the north aisle and the tower, dates back to 1859. A Bishop's Palace was built here in the 13th cen-tury and lasted for the next 300 years. When Henry VIII closed the monasteries the bishops moved to Worces-ter. Only the moat and fish ponds now remain.

The drunken vicar

Alvechurch was a wealthy church and the living was a rich one. The rector had special privileges, he was allowed to discuss matters directly with the bishop without consulting the archdeacons first.

In 1642 civil war broke out between the parliamentarians and the royal-ists. The rector at that time was William Hollington, an ardent royalist and although he was chaplain to Charles I, his home was in the village.

Following complaints from the constable of Alvechurch, Hollington was brought before the Quarter Sessions. He was accused of keeping bad company, of spending his time in public houses, of swearing and lying, of encouraging drunkenness, and of failing to curb his passions for his neigh-bour's women. Significantly, the court took no action. The constable was a parliamentarian and perhaps he was trying to get rid of Hollington.

However, when the parliamentarians won the first civil war in 1646, Hol-lington was thrown out. In his place was a well-known theologian, Richard Moore. Then Charles II was reinstated and Hollington became rector again. Moore went to Wythall chapel where his views were thought to be so outra-geous that he could only preach from the upper window of his house, Moor Green hall.

A grave matter

In the autumn of 2008 two retired ladies happened to bump into each other while walking their dogs. They stopped for a gossip and one of them told the following tale:

I saw a ghost once. I was sixteen and I'm 66 now so that's how long ago it was. I lived in Alvechurch with my mother who was a widow and very protective. I was going out with another sixteen year old, Maureen, and she kept saying to me, 'You won't be late back will you?'

We caught a bus and went to the cinema at Kings Norton. When we came out it was late and I was very worried. I kept saying, 'I won't get home on time'. She said, 'We'd better take a short cut through the churchyard'. I said, 'You know I don't like graves' and she said, 'You've no choice, you've got to do it' so we went into this churchyard.

I can't for the life of me remember whether it was a churchyard at Alvechurch or Kings Norton. It was an enormous place surrounded by a high wall. High up, near the wall, was one of the old-fashioned lamps, shining down on us. Suddenly we saw a white shape rising up out of one of the graves. It turned into a woman wearing a long white dress and it had got a mob cap on. I couldn't really tell you any more about it because it was semi-transparent. Maureen said, 'She's got a funny hat on' and with that the white lady went across the pathway and straight through the wall. We both screamed and ran.

If I'd been the only one to see it I would think it was my imagination but my friend saw it as well. Since then, I've always been interested in the paranormal. I watch all the paranormal programmes on the telly and I like reading, so I'm often reading books about it.

The graveyard at St Laurence's, Alvechurch. Fifty years ago it could have corresponded to the description above. An imaginative reconstruction of the white lady.

BARNT GREEN - A spy story

Barnt Green is one of those villages which owes its continued existence to the railway. Although its history goes back to the 1400s, the population remained tiny and in 1851 only 46 people lived there. Then, in 1859, the railway arrived. People realised that it was possible to work in the town and live in the country. Many of its residents came from two huge concerns, the Bournville chocolate factory and the Longbridge Works.

Among the older houses is the Red House, said to be haunted by the ghost of a maiden who had unhappy love affair with a young man living in a nearby Elizabethan House.

The occupant of another house in Barnt Green, John H Smith, discovered he had a notorious predecessor. Our thanks to John for providing us with a summary:

"Did you know that a spy was associated with your house?" That was the greeting from a lady who engaged me in conversation whilst working in the front garden of our house in Barnt Green. The spy in question was Alan Nunn May, Lecturer in Physics at Kings College, London, who was arrested by officers of Special Branch outside the college on the 4th March 1946. He was charged under the Official Secrets Act and remained in custody until his trial at the Old Bailey on 1st May of that year.

The name of Nunn May does not immediately spring to mind in connection with espionage. Klaus Fuchs, the Krogers, Guy Burgess, Donald Maclean and Kim Philby are more famous and were to follow in subsequent years. Who was Alan Nunn May and what happened to him?

Alan Nunn May was born in Birmingham on the 2nd May 1911, his father was a brass founder and they lived at Park Hill in Moseley. By 1914, they had moved to Blackwell Road, Barnt Green and Alan was educated at King Edward's School, Birmingham. In 1930, he went up to Trinity Hall, Cambridge to study Physics. He gained a first and at the same time became associated with communist sympathies being propounded by leading academics at Cambridge including Donald Maclean, a contemporary at Trinity Hall. It was around this time that he joined the Communist Party, but remained a somewhat shy and retiring individual. He ultimately completed a PhD there in 1936 and was appointed to a lectureship at King's College, London.

At the outbreak of war in 1939, he worked briefly on a secret radar project and then on the "Tube Alloys Project", code name for the British effort on atomic energy research. In 1944, as one of a group led by Dr

John Cockroft, he went to Canada to work on the Atomic Energy Project at Montreal. It was at this time he was approached by Russian agents. By 1945, he had supplied them with a sample of Uranium 233, and information of the first atomic test in the Alamagordo Desert, New Mexico. He received payment of 200 dollars and 2 bottles of whisky. He was later to say that he refused payment and even burnt the money but the Soviet agents retained receipts of the transactions which were to become damning indictments.

In September 1945, Nunn May returned to England and to his lectureship at King' College. However the Russian agents continued to contact him, and Colonel Zabotkin, Military Attache at the Russian Embassy in Ottawa set up a contact to meet Nunn May (code name Alek) outside the British Museum late one evening in October. Nunn May never kept that appointment and it seems he had had enough of the whole business. This would probably have brought an end to the matter, but on night of the 5th September 1945, Igor Gouzenko, a cipher clerk at the Soviet Embassy, Ottawa, defected with a number of secret files. He initially took his information to a leading newspaper but was not believed. His neighbour in the next door apartment, who happened to be a sergeant in the Canadian Air Force, did, and gave him overnight protective shelter. The Canadian authorities found themselves with "the largest and most dangerous spy plot ever known in the Dominion" and it led to numerous arrests of Canadians in the government and armed forces. Those secret files contained information related to Nunn May and were relayed to MI5 in London.

For a while M15 did nothing except to monitor Nunn May's movements, with the possibility that he may implicate others. Interestingly, Kim Philby was working with MI5 and was active as a double agent at the time. He was close to being exposed. When it was realised that no more secrets were forthcoming from M15 surveillance, Special Branch arrested Alan Nunn May at King's College in the Strand, London, on Monday 4th March 1946 when he had just finished giving a lecture.

Nunn May pleaded guilty and through his council pleaded that as a scientist he was under an obligation to see discoveries used not for a single country but for mankind as a whole. He was sentenced to 10 years in prison which was thought by many at the time to be severe but would set down a marker for those who would follow.

Nunn May was released from Wakefield Prison at the end of December 1952 having served 6 years. He eventually returned to Cambridge and married Dr Hildegarde Broda, Deputy Medical Officer of Health for Cambridge on 1st August 1953. Nunn May never revealed his Russian recruiter but files released into the public domain in 2007 hint that M15 were suspicious that this was Engelbert Broda who had divorced Hildegarde in 1946. Engelbert had worked at the Cavendish Laboratory in Cambridge with Nunn May, having fled Austria in 1938. He returned to Austria in 1948.

A few years after release from prison Nunn May secured a post as research professor in Physics in Accra at the University of Ghana. His wife went with him and she developed a reputation as a tireless medical worker in that country. Nunn May retired in 1978 and returned to live in Cambridge. He died in Cambridge on 12th January 2003.

Alan had two brothers, Ralph, and Edward who was 14 years older. Edward Nunn May had served in the 1914-18 war, became a captain and was awarded the Military Cross in the Honours list.

They were all living in the Barnt Green area during the 1939-45 war. It is interesting to speculate how the family survived a national scandal, in particular bearing in mind Edward's service in the First World War.

John is currently compiling a book on Nunn May.

BARTLEY GREEN - A little experience

The county boundaries were determined in about 918 and all kinds of peculiar anomalies were included, usually because, if the Lord of the Manor lived in this county and owned land further afield, he wanted that land included in his area of residence. An arm of Worcestershire stretches out in the northeast to Romsley, and just beyond the boundary is Bartley Green.

The village is listed in the Domesday book of 1068 but remained an obscure village until the reservoir arrived in the early 1900s. Water is carried from the Elan Valley reservoir to the one at Bartley Green ready to supply Birmingham along a 73-mile aqueduct.

Anne from Bartley Green told the following story to Ed Doolan on local radio:

I had a little experience. I used to keep an Outdoor and a lady used to come in, in the morning for her 'medicine' and this one morning she came in, looking a bit agitated. I think I must have been waiting for a delivery and she said, 'Oh, I'll come back later on'. I didn't see her again that day and her husband came in about seven o'clock, and I said to him, 'How's your wife? She seemed a bit agitated this morning'. He said, 'What time did you see her?'. I said, 'Oh, about ten o'clock'. 'I don't think so', he said. 'She died at six o'clock this morning'. And she had come in, dressed as she normally did. And that's always stuck with me.

HOLLYWOOD, The Unitarian Church, Kingswood Meeting House – The brown lady

The Unitarian church is world-wide. They have no dogma and no creed, they encourage free thought and a liberal approach to religion.. The present pastor of the Unitarian Church at Kingswood Meeting House expresses his beliefs in the following quotation by A S Maney: ' ... we should have a concern for, and be ready to offer kindness and help to any folk who are in need or distress. Only on such a basis can human life be lived well and happily. Love is the law of life.'

The early Unitarians probably fled from Birmingham in about 1708 to escape persecution, building a meeting house in Dark Lane, Hollywood. No doubt they hoped to be able to worship in peace, but unfortunately that was not to be. The chapel had only been standing for seven years when it damaged by rioters. One of the arsonists was hung at Worcester Assizes. The chapel was repaired but in 1791 rioters succeeded in burning the chapel to the ground. Undeterred, the congregation set about building a new chapel hidden away in Packhorse Lane. It was completed in 1793.

The Reverend Keith Hill was minister there for 40 years but has now retired. He says:

It's a very interesting churchyard. A mayor of Birmingham is buried here, also a member of the Baldwin family and there are three war graves. Two were RAF pilots - Jephot was the name of one of them, he was killed at the end of May 1945. The third war grave is for Reverend Bull. Although he had lived here for many years, he had been in the American services.

One of the Kinder children is buried in the churchyard. She came over from Germany during the persecution of the Jews and lived in Moseley but unfortunately a bomb dropped on her house and she was killed. After the war her mother, who had been in a concentration camp but survived, came to England to try to find her. This year the Jewish organisation came over to hold a service in the churchyard.

As for the ghost, I haven't seen it but two organists have seen it. The new minister's partner has also seen it and was freaked out by it. Apparently, it was a brown lady.

Reverend Hill's wife, Jo, tells the story:

I was in the church. Beryl (a church member) turned to me and said, 'It's hot in here'. I said, 'No. I've gone stone cold'. I was coming out of the church and two people said to me, 'Did you see it?'. I said, 'See what?'. They said, 'The brown lady. She was standing there looking at you'.

The Unitarian Church at Kingswood Meeting House.

Why me? I expected to kick the bucket or something the next week. My coat was like an ice block. Anthony (the minister) went cold as well but he didn't see anything.

However, when I first went to the church, I was in the church by myself and I could hear thousands of voices, as if everybody who had been there in the past was there.

Peter Flower has been the organist for about eighteen months.

I was here one evening practising. The church was empty and everything was quiet. I became aware of somebody sitting towards the back of the church. I had locked the front doors so anyone coming in would have to enter through the side doors and walk past me, and I knew no-one had come in. I had heard stories about the brown lady who sometimes pays a visit but I had never taken much notice, and so I guessed this was the lady in question. She looked like a real person. She wasn't scary at all, she just sat there. She was very elderly, I would say in her eighties, with grey hair and a brown coat done up very tightly up to her neck. After a couple of minutes, she just went.

Marina and her daughter, Nina, prepare the refreshments, such as the tea and coffee after each meeting on a Sunday. Marina says:

We have no idea who the ghost is. We have both sensed her, you feel as if someone is behind you but when you turn round no-one is there. I have only seen her once and that was about a few weeks ago.

29

We were sitting in a service and I felt someone behind me so I turned round to see if anyone was there and a lady was walking down the aisle. She was middle-aged and wearing a black cape, with the hood up. Rather stupidly I thought, 'Oh, it's pouring with rain, that's why she's got her coat on'. She went past the back three rows, then she disappeared.

WYTHALL – the haunted iPod

Many people are surprised to learn that Wythall is in Worcestershire. The village lies on both sides of the A435 Alcester to Birmingham Road. It has one of F W Preedy's churches, built in 1862, and has at last achieved fame with the arrival of the Transport Museum.

Two lovely ladies from Wythall decided to celebrate New Year 2008/9 by taking a holiday at the seaside resort of Eastbourne:

I think I should start at the beginning. I went to Eastbourne with a friend in the New Year that's just gone. On the way down my friend asked me if I wanted to listen to her iPod but I said, 'No'.

We stayed in a large Victorian house near the theatre where I was sharing a room with my friend. That night, when we were ready for bed, I drew the curtains and where I had drawn the curtains there was a bright green florescent light all down the one edge of the curtain on the left-hand side. I thought it was a security light or something on the outside of the building and I didn't think much about it. My friend also saw it.

Two days later I was getting ready to go down to dinner and I was late getting dressed so I sent my friend on down. My case was underneath the curtain on a chair and the chair was next to the wardrobe. My friend's jacket was hanging in the wardrobe. I had my back to the wardrobe when suddenly I heard this horrible demonic laughter coming from over my shoulder. It was like something out of a horror film. It wasn't a man's deep voice, more I would say, from someone aged between 30 and 40, an impish sound. As soon as I reached the wardrobe the laughter stopped so I would say that it went on for about half a minute. I guessed the iPod was in my friend's pocket and I assumed my friend had recorded something on her iPod to frighten me for a joke. In fact, I wasn't frightened, I felt quite calm about it. I went down to dinner and I thought, 'I won't mention it'. We ate our meal and I forgot all about it.

Next day I heard the demonic laughter again when I was standing in the same spot. I thought she had put the iPod on as before and had left it ready as a joke. I thought 'That thing's come on again'. As the previous evening, I went down to the meal and forgot all about it.

On the way home I said, 'You set that thing up in the bedroom to frighten me but I wasn't frightened'. It was obvious that she didn't know what I was talking about. When I explained, she said it was impossible for the iPod to make a noise as the battery had run out.

That reminded me, I had another strange experience there. I went to the toilet one night and the bedroom floor was bathed in light. I thought, 'There's me, feeling my way all round the bedroom in the dark and the floor is all lit up'. I assumed it was the light from the corridor coming in under the door. You know what these hotel doors are like, there's usually a crack along the bottom of the door where the light comes in from the corridor but when I think about it, there was only a tiny crack under the door and the floor was flooded with light.

JKP

4. BEWDLEY

his attractive little town situated on the river Severn owes its beauty to both its riches and its poverty. From mediaeval times to 1711 Bewdley was one of the great Midland ports. Goods such as wool, porcelain, coal and wood came and went on the river Severn between Birmingham, Bristol, London and the whole of the Midlands. The streets were lined with fine buildings such as the George Hotel which features later in this chapter

The boundary between Shropshire and Worcestershire was uncertain at Bewdley with the result that it was a haven for criminals. If a felon was arrested by the bailiffs of one county he could claim to have come from the other county so that they had no jurisdiction over him. Bewdley belonged to Edward IV and when he became king in 1461 honours were heaped upon the town with the additional privilege of becoming a sanctuary town. The old names are still in use, there is Catchem's End, the last point at which a wrongdoer could be arrested, and Whispering Street, where miscreants waited for darkness to fall so that they could reach sanctuary. It is said that the virtuous lived near the river and the criminal element lived on the edge of the town so that they could not be caught and dragged beyond sanctuary. Bewdley ceased to be a sanctuary town in 1536 during the reign of Henry VIII and was firmly placed in Worcestershire in 1544. To a certain extent, law and order was restored.

In the mid 18th century, Bewdley's fortunes took a dramatic change. The building of Stourport-on-Severn took their trade from them. Contemporary

Bewdley bridge, built by Thomas Telford (1757-1834). He built 900 miles of road and over 100 bridges.

historians tell of 400 donkeys standing idle. The wealth of the town came to an end. There was no money to rebuild or develop but this has had the happy result that the town has remained an early eighteenth century gem.

Tickenhill and the Spanish princess

Not only was Bewdley a great trading centre, a Royal Palace, Tickenhill, stood on the edge of the town, one of the seats of the powerful Council of the Welsh Marches. This brought royal visitors who stabled their horses at the local inns and sometimes lodged there, entertained by travelling players and musicians. For several months, the tragic Catherine of Aragon lived at Tickenhill and it was here that she was betrothed by proxy to the twelve-year old Prince Arthur, the eldest son of Henry VIII. Sadly, Prince Arthur died at the age of sixteen only five months after the official wedding. Catherine of Aragon was too good a prize to lose, so she was then married to Arthur's younger brother, Henry, later to become Henry VIII, despite the fact that she was older by five-and-a-half years. Catherine bore him about six children but only one survived, Mary. It was to Tickenhill that Princess Mary came while her father was going through divorce proceedings. She originally arrived with a household of 250 but after the divorce her household was reduced, and she wrote to Henry asking if 69 of the poorest servants could be found places in various religious houses.

Princess Mary was crowned queen in 1553 when she was 37 years of age. Unfortunately, she believed that the way to deal with those who did not conform to her beliefs, was to burn them and she became known as 'Bloody Mary'. She only ruled for five years before she died.

Tickenhill fell into disrepair and was pulled down in 1738. A nursing home now stands on the site.

The Bewdley Election Scandal

Stanley Baldwin was elected prime minister three times, in 1908, 1923 and 1935. Bewdley have claimed him as their own but in actual fact he lived for most of his life at Wilden near Stourport-on-Severn and his retirement was spent at Astley Hall.

Not everyone knows that his father, Alfred Baldwin, was involved in a political scandal in 1869, so severe that he retired from politics for several years and instead, concentrated on developing the large iron works that he owned at Wilden.

Before 1832 parliamentary seats tended to passed down through families, rather like hereditary titles. Then the system was revised so that about three people in every hundred were eligible to vote. Of course, these three were very important. Voting was not in secret until 14 years later, so everyone knew where their loyalties lay. They were bribed, threatened, even kidnapped. In about 1850, several Bewdley supporters who probably would have voted Liberal were spirited away to Stanford Bridge, entertained with fishing, eating and drinking and kept under surveillance until voting had closed.

In another Act of 1867, men were allowed to vote if they owned or rented property worth about £10 or £12 a year. Although this only included about seven out of every hundred men, at least it was a step forward. There was great excitement. Bribery and corruption was made illegal, but it had not disappeared.

In the elections of 1868, Alfred Baldwin was supporting Mr Lloyd, a Liberal (the old 'Whig' party) , against Sir Richard Glass, a Conservative (the old Tory). Generally speaking, the Liberals supported the workers and the Conservatives the ruling classes. Sir Richard was about 48 years of age and had made his money through the manufacture of telegraph cables. His election campaign was as follows:

On 6th July Sir Richard came to the town to canvas and was welcomed by the firing of canons. First he went to the house of a local solicitor who gave free refreshments to everyone including an entire barrel of beer. He continued to the Peacock Inn where he gave a sovereign (£1 – a lot of money in those days) for free beer, then to the Packhorse Inn, where the local doctor, Dr Webster, treated everyone to free beer.

Sir Richard stayed at Lickhill for a few days. During that period he visited a total of 33 pubs. On one occasion he said, 'Drink away boys, it's the Whigs want to stop you from having your ale'. As many as 100 people were often crammed into these little pubs. Some wives brought jugs and put the jugs under the taps then took the beer home. Sometimes the licensee tried to stop the tap but the drinkers turned nasty and so more beer had to be provided. At the Pack Horse, locals drank 100 gallons. As well as free beer, the Old Mug House and the Swan were supplying free tobacco, brought in on a saucer. Sir Richard also called in at a tanner's yard and left them two cans of beer - each can held ten gallons.

For the election, Mr Danks, a local barge owner, brought in men who were eligible to vote from Bristol and Gloucester, giving them free rides on his barges and plying them with drink on the way.

Even the police supported this munificence and channelled people into the public houses where free beer was being offered. The landlord of The Fox was a well-known Liberal. He was ill and when Dr Webster (Conservative) came to see him, he gave him Sir Richard's card and asked the publican

Load Street in Bewdley, the town's main thoroughfare. The George Hotel is on the right, halfway along the line of buildings.

to vote for Sir Richard. While the doctor was upstairs, one of his supporters said to his wife, 'That's a pretty paper in the fireplace' and as she looked at the fireplace he pressed five shillings (25p) into her hand.

One of the Liberal supporters, Mr Radnor, had been out of work for some months and he was promised a month's work if he voted for Sir Richard.

At each election 'watchers' were appointed as stewards and they were supposed to ensure that no-one received 'a treat'. However, in this small town, between 100 and 200 watchers were appointed, most of them by Sir Richard's supporters. If a watcher received a payment he was not eligible to vote for six months but most of them voted. The watchers were taken one by one into a darkened room to be paid and the man who handed them their money was wearing a mask and a wig. They received three shillings for a day's work and five shillings for a night's work.

Sir Richard won the election but Alfred Baldwin reported him for bribery and corruption.

The press loved it. The editor of *Berrows Worcester Journal* wrote, '*The Telegraph* revelled in the subject, the *Birmingham Post* could not conceal its joy and the *Chronicle*, while rejoicing in the result ... described Bewdley as a peasant borough where corruption is ingrained'.

In January 1869, Rt Hon Colin Blackburn QC came to Bewdley to hear the case. Reporters were at the station several hours before his train was due. They expected him to arrive in robe and wig and were surprised to see an ordinary-looking man alight from the train.

It turned out that the Liberal Mr Lloyd was not squeaky clean either. There had been a rally at the Anchor at which over 150 were present and several ten-gallon cans of beer had been brought in and distributed.

The judge in his summing up said that Sir Richard had distributed his treats to everyone, not just the Conservatives, therefore he could not be accused of bribery and corruption. If his supporters had been over-enthusiastic that was not his fault. There was no blemish on his character.

John Blome was hanged

The George Hotel was the most important inn of one of England's major ports and it still dominates the main street through the town. In its coaching days it could stable over forty horses. Inquests and courts were held here, and it also probably served as the local lock-up. On a window in an upper floor is scratched, 'John Blome, 1777, March 4, was hanged'. The George has been frequented by the cream of society. The royal visitors to Tickenhill came in the 15th and 16th century, Charles I stayed here in 1645 during the English civil war and Charles de Gaulle during World War II.

The ballroom, with its ornate fireplace and wonderful chandeliers, has now been converted into a ladies' room and this where the traditional ghost, the grey lady, is said to walk at night.

Left: The George Hotel.
Below: The ghost in the mirror of the old ballroom.

So many strange events have taken place recently that a team from Parasearch, who specialise in investigating the paranormal, was called in and took the unusual step of inviting the public to spend an all-night vigil with them. About fifty people assembled at midnight on Sunday, 2nd October 2008 to be divided into groups. Each group spent half-an-hour sitting in the dark in a certain area, watching and listening, before moving to another area for a further half-hour. Cameras and a whole range of delicate instruments instruments were put in place. The vigil lasted until 5.30 am.

Between each session there was a short break, when staff members talked about various strange incidents that had taken place recently:

One member of staff said:

A colleague of ours, Charlotte, was clearing out the bins in the ladies' toilets in the converted ballroom. She came out of the last toilet and began to wash her hands in one of the basins by the basins. She happened to glance over at the large mirror by the shower and saw, in the mirror, the ghost of a little girl standing by the big fireplace, watching her. Charlotte said that she saw the little girl quite clearly, she was somewhere between seven or eleven and was wearing old-fashioned clothes. Charlotte was quite calm about it, she just walked out of the room.

The bartender reported:

A few days ago, a guest was staying in one of our rooms with his son. He got up first thing in the morning and was surprised to see the curtains opening on their own. I was working behind the bar and he came down to tell me about it. He was quite surprised. His son had seen them open as well.

Another of our staff, Emma, was doing the housekeeping. She was in the only room with a table. She was stripping down the bed sheet when she saw an old gentleman sitting in a chair next to the table. He was red-faced and was wearing a waistcoat and plus-fours. She couldn't get out of the room quickly enough! After that she left and went back to college.

Another staff member says:

We have CCTV evidence of the ghost. There's a large table next to the kitchen and a couple of weeks ago one of our staff was clearing the table. The bar was fully open and a number of people were in the room. When we looked at the CCTV footage, we saw a grey shape walk round the table.

The report from Parasearch shows that, during the night, the most inexplicable activity came from the ballroom. There were footsteps coming from vacant areas, cold draughts, unusual noises and increases in magnetic fields. The lower bar area was also subject to similar inexplicable activity.

The Bewdley Ghost Train
by David Taylor, Chairman of Parasearch

Stories of ghost trains are a unique aspect of ghost lore, with many books and even films featuring them. Reports of ghost trains in Worc estershire are few and far between, so the following report from Bewdley is very interesting.

We shall call the witness Vincent, although this is not his real name. Sometime during the summer of 2004 he and four friends were in Northwood Lane, Bewdley, at around 2.30am. They had been out for the evening, and it was common for them to drive out to an isolated spot afterwards. They were parked at the end of North-wood Lane where the Elan Valley aqueduct passes under the rail-way line. When they arrived they were surprised to see they were not alone – a VW camper van was already there. Its occupants said they were there to see the ghost train! Thinking this would be worth the wait, Vincent and his friends decided to settle down and wait.

After a while they all heard the tracks rattling and what they de-scribed as a 'heat haze' moving along the track travelling in the di-rection of Bewdley from Bridgnorth. There appeared to be smoke coming out of the top where the engine's funnel should be. They watched in amazement as an estimated 5-6 carriages passed them by at close quarters. Once the strange spectral sight had vanished from view the witnesses sat in their respective vehicles in shock.

Parasearch investigators George Gregg, Russell Beard and Andrew Homer interviewed the witness and visited Northwood Lane. They could find no natural explanation for the sighting. Parasearch member Dave Walker was able to suggest contacting SVR Marketing Manager John Leach to see if he had heard any reports of a spectral train in the area. At the same time Parasearch Chairman David Taylor was researching the area. What he found out backed up the information supplied by John Leach.

In 1976 the SVR was used by the BBC for a TV adaptation of 'The Signalman' for their successful 'Ghost Story for Christmas'. The ghost story, by Charles Dickens, first published in 1866 tells the sto-ry of a ghost that has been haunting a lonely railway signalman. For their dramatisation the BBC used the Severn Valley Railway for their filming. It is the belief of Parasearch that this was the genesis of the Bewdley ghost train story, and would explain why, when Vincent and friends arrived at Northwood Lane, people were already there to see the ghost train. This, combined with night time freight trains may help to explain one of Worcestershire few ghost train reports.

However, it doesn't end there, for perhaps Northwood Lane is truly haunted. One local resident believes it is. Simon (not his real name) was returning home late one night down the dark lane. Behind him he heard the distinctive sound of someone running on the hard surface. He stepped to one side to let them pass – but there was no one there! He was all alone! So next time you are in Bewdley, keep an eye and an ear open ...

A walking weekend brings a surprise

Living in the Bewdley area are a group of friends comprising five or six married couples. The men all once worked for the same company and both husbands and wives have since remained friends. One of them, Steven, organises entertainment and events. He will ring them all up and ask if they would like to go on a theatre trip or a holiday somewhere. On the weekend of 14th June, 1993, he organised a walking weekend for eight of them, with two nights half board at The Manor in Stanton, south of Broadway. One member of the party was Doreen, who was delighted with the venue. She says:

It's a lovely mediaeval manor, given by Henry VIII to Catherine Parr as a wedding gift. It was absolutely beautiful, with antique furniture. Henry VIII is supposed to have slept there and there's a room with a four-poster bed in it known as the King's room, said to be a replica of the one Henry VIII slept in. A nice couple ran it, they were very welcoming.

We went to bed on the Saturday night in a lovely old-fashioned room. I was in a double bed with my husband. I'm a light sleeper, I don't go to sleep easily. Whether I had been to sleep or not I don't know but I wanted to go to the loo in the night. I went to get out of bed when I saw 'her' coming out of the wardrobe. I thought, 'That's strange, somebody coming out of the wardrobe'. She was dressed as a Puritan, with a white collar and a white cap. Her dress was in two different shades of grey, a lighter grey with a dark piece on it, She was about 30 or 35 years of age, tall and slim, quite solid and so clear. Her cap covered her head and I could see how her cap curved down the side of her face. Her arms were hanging down with her hands clasped together in front of her. She didn't look at all frightening, she looked very peaceful and serene and was looking down with a very calm expression. She was very gentle in appearance, perhaps that's why she didn't startle me. I wasn't at all frightened. I just thought, 'That's a queer dress'.

She was there for several seconds, she walked towards me, across the whole length of the room. I didn't wake my husband, I don't know why. I was fascinated; I just sat and watched her. I expected her to fade away but when she was only about a yard away (nearly a metre) I closed my eyes to check that I wasn't dreaming and when I opened them she wasn't there. The next morning I looked behind the wardrobe with my husband and there was an archway, it looked as if a door had been there at some time.

We went down to an excellent breakfast on the Sunday morning. Our hostess, Pat, asked if anyone had seen anything during the night. Evidently the place was known to be haunted and sometime previously one of the guests had seen a crinoline lady. My lady wasn't wearing a crinoline. I didn't say anything at first, I don't know why I didn't, then I told everyone.

Pat didn't tell us that the place was haunted until the Sunday morning, so I hadn't gone to bed expecting to see a ghost.

That's the one and only time that I have seen a ghost.

5. THE BROMSGROVE AREA

he ancient town of Bromsgrove developed on a prehistoric trackway from Worcester northwards through Droitwich, and was a place of some importance in William the Conqueror's Domesday Book of 1086. During the 16th and 17th centuries Bromsgrove was the world centre for nail manufacturing and grew rapidly, by 1770 the town had 400 houses. During the 1800s nail-making was the principal trade of the town but by 1900, the trade had died out.

The town is also well known for a group of artists known as 'The Bromsgrove Guild' They created wood carvings, jewellery, metalwork and stained glass. One of their most famous works is the gates of Buckingham Palace. Their work is now highly prized and a recent pair of urns were sold recently for nearly £5,000.

One of Britain's finest independent schools is here, Bromsgrove School, founded in 1533 by Henry VIII. Many of its pupils have become famous world-wide such as the poet Alfred Housman who wrote 'The Shropshire Lad'. His statue stands in the town centre.

Some investigators into the paranormal would argue that the great age of the town is the reason why so many of Bromsgrove's shops appear to be haunted. The 'Stone Tape' theory suggests that bricks and stones can hold a recording of past events which can be played back by certain people. Shop assistants complain of articles mysteriously disappearing and turning up in weird places, of the sound of footsteps coming from empty rooms, and often, they hear someone come into the shop but when go to serve the customer, no-one is there.

Was I mistaken?

A short distance from the centre of the town, is number 165A Birmingham Road, a grim red-bricked building. This is the old workhouse, built in 1836 to take the poor and needy from twelve parishes and used as such until 1901. Families were separated, husbands from wives, children from parents. The building was nicknamed 'The Bastille'. In 1878 a workhouse hospital was built behind it which, after various uses, was demolished to make way for the Princess of Wales Community Hospital, built in 1992.

Until recent years, 165A Birmingham Road was the headquarters of the Bromsgrove and Redditch Health Authority known as 'The Path Lab' because of a small annex on the right used as a pathology laboratory. It had the reputation of being haunted. One morning in about1986, the domestic supervisor opened a broom cupboard on the top floor to find the ghost of an elderly gentleman sitting there. The domestic staff had had so many other frights that they gave in their notices en masse. The General Manager said that if they stayed on, they need not start work before 9 am when all the office staff were present. The building has now been converted into offices.

These strange experiences also seem to have affected the area outside. A local lady, Diane says:

About twenty years ago, I was walking along the road by the old workhouse one morning, on my way to visit my grandma, when I bumped into an old lady that I knew, outside her house. I said, 'Hullo' and she smiled. The next day I heard from a lady that she had died the day before I saw her. The lady asked me if I could have been mistaken but told her I was sure I wasn't, I knew the old lady well. I have always believed in that sort of thing so I wasn't altogether surprised.

The ghosts of Barnsley Hall

About a mile further north the Birmingham Road is crossed by the M42 and just to the south west was Barnsley Hall. The Barnsley family were in Bromsgrove as far back as the 1400s but in 1771, the hall was pulled down and a large farm built. The 324-acre site was bought by Bromsgrove Council and a hospital opened there in 1907. Although its proper name was 'Bromsgrove Lunatic Asylum' it was always known as 'Barnsley Hall Hospital'. At the outbreak of the Second World War, three wards were taken over and thirty new wards were erected in the grounds. Barnsley Hall became one of the largest emergency hospitals in the county taking a variety of

165A B'ham Road, 'The Path Lab'.

casualties including air-raid victims and men from the Front. Few people realise how large this complex was, the hospital behind 165A and Barnsley Hall combined could take 500 patients.

George Gregg, a psychiatric nurse, worked in the hospital between 1979 and 1990. He says:

The hospital had the reputation of being haunted. The old school of nursing was creepy especially on the top floor. It was more obvious when I was working late on my own, There was a sense of presence in the place. All kinds of rumours reached my ears. In the elderly care wards nurses could hear footsteps going to the toilet. I heard that a night sister who passed away in the 1960s used to put in an appearance from time to time in one of the female wards.

One morning, around 1982, I was told about a 'strange experience' that had occurred during the handover by the night staff. The staff nurse said that patients were asleep and the wards were in semi-darkness, the only light being in the office where the staff were working. Except for an occasional snore or a quiet muttering by one of the patients in their sleep, all was silent. It was about 3.00am when there was a sudden blinding flash of light accompanied with a tremendous explosion somewhere outside the hospital. The nurse in charge dropped her pen and rushed to the door. She thought that a gas main must have exploded somewhere. Several other staff were in the corridor, staring about, saying, 'What was that?'. They looked around for an explanation and in the morning the porters and nursing officer made a careful investigation outside, but nothing was ever found to explain such an inexplicable phenomena. The general opinion of those staff who had experienced the mystery explosion, was that it must have been a UFO!

Rex G Wise, in the 1987 *Rousler*, says that one night, all the patients were in bed and they went into the kitchen to make a cup of tea. The door at the top of the dormitory opened and closed and they heard footsteps. The key turned in the lock and the door leading to the steps of 'O' ward opened and closed. The nurse opened the door and saw a figure in Edwardian clothes making her way down the steps to 'O' ward.

Barnsley Hall has now been demolished and a housing estate is on the site.

A rude awakening

The following story was told at an antique collectors' fair held in Bromsgrove market hall in December 2008:

Four or five years ago I was having an afternoon nap and I woke up to find a young woman standing by the side of my bed. She smiled and I blinked because I couldn't believe my eyes – how could anyone have got in the house? – then she was gone. She looked as solid as you or me. She was wearing fairly modern clothes, about 1930s or 40s, a skirt and a striped blouse. I would say she was between 40 and 45 and she had light brown hair.

I wondered if she had slipped out. I got up and tried the front and back doors but they were both locked. I thought she might be hiding in the house and I looked everywhere but she wasn't there.

I didn't believe in ghosts until then.

The fey child

Marjorie was originally from Liverpool but has lived in Bromsgrove for many years.

I do believe there is something else after death. We have a lot of unusual things happening with my grand-daughter. When she was little she used to talk to someone at night. We used to say to her, 'Who are talking to, love? She would say, 'That lady at the end of the bed'. We asked her to describe her to us. She said that the lady had long grey hair, long dangly earrings, lots of jewellery and she described her long dress. We used to have an aged hippy living next door to us and that described her 'to a T'. She had died before my grand-daughter was born.

One day, she wanted to go to see her aunty's house, a short distance away. She'd never been there but she knew the way better than I did. When we got there she said, 'Oh, it's changed'. She described it as having a red door and roses up the wall. That's how it used to be.

Strange things happen in our house when she's around. She took a plate into the kitchen to wash, put it in the sink and when she turned round it was on the table again. The same with a book. She put it away and then a second later it was back on the table. It was most bizarre.

The visitor

By a strange coincidence, here is another story about a 'fey'child. The para-psychologist working with with Parasearch advises that the parents should simply treat this is normal and take no specific action.

Unfortunately, my marriage broke up and so in about 1995 I moved to a Victorian house about two miles outside Brornsgrove with my two daughters. My youngest daughter said that a lady used to come into her

room. Her description of the lady was so consist-
ent we knew she was telling the truth. My daughter said that she was a pleasant-looking lady, she
used to smile at her and walk away. She looked as
if she was going to a May-day celebration, her hair
was up and there was a circlet of flowers in her hair.
From her description, the dress was Edwardian.

I remarried in 2003 and my husband came to
live with us. He never felt comfortable in the
house. He always felt that he was being watched
and sometimes, he could hear somebody calling
him. He could also hear someone running up and
down the stairs. The kitchen had an old-fashioned
door with a lock and key and on a couple of occasions he went into the kitchen and found that he was locked in.

I didn't see anything but I would hear footsteps going up and down
the stairs. Perhaps it helped that I knew the couple who lived there
before us and they were a lovely old couple. If anything unusual happened, I just used to say, 'Hullo'.

The hovering visor

This is the first time that a haunted visor has been reported.

We have a ghost in our house in Bromsgrove. We can hear someone moving about upstairs and we hear bumps and bangs. I have felt
somebody sitting by my leg when nobody is there. One evening, we
sat watching the telly and all of a sudden, an old-fashioned visor appeared in mid-air, hovered, then dropped onto the floor. My wife and
I just looked at each other. We still have it.

Things move or disappear. To take one example, my wife's wedding ring disappeared. She put it on the shelf together with her engagement ring while she did some gardening. When she came back in
the evening her engagement ring was still there but the wedding ring
had gone. In the end, we bought another one. Then five months later,
she moved a picture off the shelf and there it was, where she had put
it. That picture had been moved many times.

When my two lads were about six we went fishing. When we came
back all the bottles in the bathroom were lying on their side in the
middle of the floor. The boys said, 'What's the point of doing that?'. I
told them, 'I haven't done it!'.

I kept smelling a heavy sweet perfume, like lavender. You would smell it, it would disappear for a while then you would be able to smell it again.

One night, I saw an old lady. She had grey hair permed very tight to her head and a flowery dress. I would say she went back to the 1960s or 70s. I saw her several times, I mentioned it one night and my son said that he had seen the same lady. He had been sitting on his bed, combing his hair, and he saw her go past in the mirror with the same smell and everything. When I spoke to our next door neighbour, he said his mum used to live in our house and she looked just like that. She wore the same kind of perfume.

The haunted highway

Most of the A448 Bromsgrove Highway is a new road but, at the Bromsgrove end and near the exit for Finstall, the highway joins the old road. Many phantoms have been seen here. The *Redditch Advertiser* of 5 December 1990 had the headline 'Highway horror from the ghoul' and stated that the phantom always appears in a long cloak. The road would have been used by the monks and lay brothers of Bordesley Abbey as nearby Hewell Grange was one of their farms or granges.

Young Neil saw yet another ghost in 2008:

I was on the Bromsgrove Highway, near where the train bridge goes over the road. It was about 10 pm at night and the heater was full on. I noticed that about ten or twenty feet away on the side of the road was a woman with a long black veil over her head and feet. I could only see her shape and I could tell that she wasn't real because she was hovering. She started to move towards the road and came on to the verge. As I went past the spot the car went icy cold, although the heater was full on. After I had gone past, it warmed up.

HANBURY – Scandals at Hanbury Hall

Worcestershire stately homes have few scandals to tell as most of the mansions were occupied by pious Roman Catholic families whose worst sin was to try to blow up the Houses of Parliament. However, the Vernon family at Hanbury Hall have provided us with a number of memorable episodes.

The first member of the Vernon family to live in Hanbury was Richard Vernon in 1580 who was appointed Rector of Hanbury. He lived at Astwood Farm and bought Spernal Hall in 1596. His great grandson was Sir Thomas Vernon, one of the king's barristers and a leading counsellor in Chancery. The recent scandals of public figures lining their pockets at the expense of the general public are nothing compared to the wealth accumulated by Sir Thomas. He reckoned that he had earned £112,000, an enormous fortune in those days. In 1701 he rebuilt Spernal Hall employing one of the best artists of the day, Sir James Thornhill, who decorated the walls and ceilings. This new mansion was renamed Hanbury Hall.

Sir Thomas had no family and the estate passed to his cousin, Bowater Vernon. His granddaughter, Emma Vernon succeeded in 1772 when she was only sixteen years of age. About four years later she was married to Henry Cecil, a descendent of one of Queen Elizabeth's favourites and nephew and heir to the ninth earl of Exeter. Both Henry Cecil and Emma Vernon were wild young things.

Emma lived chiefly at Hanbury, while her husband was usually in London. A lonely Emma became friendly with the local curate, William Sneyde and to everyone's amazement, they ran away together, ending up in Portugal. Henry Cecil knew he would be the laughing stock of all London so he changed his name to John Jones and went to live in rural Shropshire. He wasn't squeaky clean either as he bigamously married Sarah Hoggins, a farmer's daughter. The tale is told that Sarah knew nothing of his inheritance and was amazed when Cecil's uncle died and he became Lord Burghley. She was known as 'the Cottage Countess' and was very well-known, books, poems and even an oratorio, have been written or composed in her honour.

As for Emma, her beloved curate died of consumption. She returned to Hanbury Hall but under the laws of the day, all her property now belonged to her husband. She turned to a local solicitor to sort out her affairs which he did, by marrying her, and they lived frugally in Hanbury Hall. When Emma knew she had not long to live, she sent for a maid and asked her to be sure that when she was buried, she was wrapped in the blanket in which she had nursed her beloved curate. She asked to be buried, not in the family vault, but in unconsecrated ground. Since then, the churchyard has been enlarged so that she now lies on its northern edge.

The hall passed down the family and was eventually inherited by Sir Harry Foley Vernon MP, who was squire for over 60 years and respected by all. Unfortunately, his son, who became squire in 1920, did not follow in his father's footsteps. In *The Lost World of Hanbury*, the authors state that Sir George Vernon, 'was more like the villainous and lustful squire in so many Victorian melodramas'.

In 1905 he married Doris Allan, daughter of James Allan who owned the Allan Shipping Line. One day, she went into her husband's room to find the maid sitting on his knee. She packed her bags and went to live at her mother's home in Shrawley Wood. When the author went to Hanbury to research the Vernon family, a group of local people told her that, once a week, Sir George went to the local school to teach religious education, and a number of pupils in each class were his spitting image.

Then came the affair of Sir George and his secretary. Ruth Powick was the daughter of the Foreman of the Vernon estate, she left school at 13 and went to work at the Hall. When she was 16 and Sir George was about 61, he asked her father if he could borrow her for six months, saying that affairs were in a mess at the Hall. He sent her off to learn shorthand and typing and she became his secretary. Ten years later, he told her father that he was leaving everything to her in his will and asked permission to change her name by deed poll to Vernon. From then on, he introduced her everywhere as his adopted daughter.

However, Sir George had his good points. He took an interest in local events and he was Chairman of the local Ratepayer's Association which monitored the rates to make sure that they were fair and accurate. Over the years, he had refused to pay the tithes on his land claimed by the church. Some were due on land he had given to the church to enlarge the graveyard! The bailiffs laid a claim on pieces of his furniture, so, what he did, was to build a small platform outside his house and hold a public auction of the furniture in question!

Sir George ended his life in 1940 with a grand finale, shooting himself in the Blue Room of Hanbury Hall, although he did take his false teeth out first. No-one is sure why he took such drastic action, perhaps he was going to be interned because he supported the Birmingham fascist, Sir Oswald Mosley, or perhaps, at 74 years of age, he had health worries. Sir George had refused to have a Christian burial. He once announced at a public meeting,

Hanbury Hall in the time of Sir George.

48

'No snivelling parson is going to read anything over me'. He was buried in the garden of his favourite cottage at Shrawley, overlooking Middle Pool. The cottage is now a ruin but the sandstone grave is still there.

Ruth inherited both the Hanbury and the Shrawley estates but not the hall and garden as these had been settled on Lady Doris by her father many years previously, and Sir George had bequeathed the hall to the National Trust. Lady Doris moved into the Hall where she lived in two rooms in penury, with a one-bar electric fire for heating. Ruth moved to the house at Shrawley, taking with her the furniture from Hanbury Hall and she later married an engineer, Frederick Horton. Lady Doris died in 1962.

The ghost of Emma Vernon

Nearly every collection of ghost stories contains a sighting of the ghost of Emma Vernon. She has been seen right across Hanbury, as far as the Country Girl where, in the 1970s, visitors came out from Birmingham in the hope of catching a glimpse of the ghost. In 1982 a bellringer was locking up when a white shape drifted up the drive and through the great Church doors. He was very shaken.

A first-hand account comes from a lady who lives nearby. She says,

I had always pooh-poohed the stories of the ghost of Emma Vernon then one morning, when I was taking my two dogs for a walk up to Hanbury Church at about eleven o'clock, I saw a dark figure with a cloak disappear round the other side of the church. I thought, 'Somebody is up to no good' and I let the dogs off the lead and ran

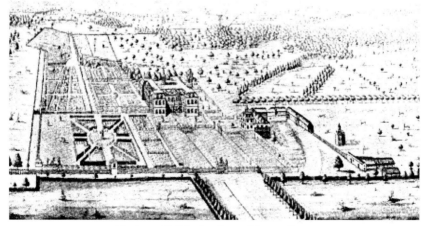

Hanbury Hall in the time of Emma Vernon.

49

to the back of the church. No-one was there, you can see for miles around and no-one was running away, in any case, the dogs would have chased them.

BENTLEY - The black dog of Bentley

By another strange co-incidence we have yet another 'dog' story.
Halfway between Bromsgrove and the southern tip of Redditch are the hamlets of Bentley, Upper and Lower, an area much favoured by the gentry and aristocracy in times past. In 1714 Sir Cookes, founder of Worcestershire College at Oxford was living at Bentley Manor. During the next century it was purchased by a master needlemaker and farmer, Walter Hemming, and until the first World War it was occupied by a descendent of the founder, Mrs Grey-Cheape. Then it was occupied by the forces. After the war it fell into disrepair and was eventually demolished.

The lady telling this creepy story has now moved nearer to Birmingham:
If my mother had lived she would now be in her nineties. Before Bentley Manor was knocked down, she lived in Bentley. During her childhood she had lived in both Lower Bentley and Upper Bentley farmhouses, and I can't remember which one had the apparition, but I think it was Lower Bentley.

At that point in time the toilets were down in the grounds of the farm. Whenever one of the family had to go in the night they always tried to take someone with them because a black dog dragging a chain used to come out of the wall of the privy. My mother saw it and her mother and various cousins. It was seen very regularly, perhaps weekly. Because it was a common occurrence, they weren't all that bothered by it, but they tended to think there was safety in numbers. When two of them went, they both would see it, however, my grandfather never saw it, all the years that he lived there.

Bentley is not the only place to have been haunted by a black dog. About 4 miles away (6km) are the Bordesley Abbey meadows haunted by the Black Dog of Arden. (See the chapter on Redditch).

In years gone by, the sighting of a black dog was said to be a warning of an impending death. An elderly lady at Cookhill always maintained that she saw such a ghost leaving her kitchen just before her brother died.

BURCOT- A miscellany of ghosts

Although Burcot is only a small village two miles north-east of Bromsgrove, it has had the honour of appearing in William the Conqueror's Domesday

book of 1086 under the name of Bericote. It's situated near the Lickey in-
cline, the steepest main line railway gradient in Great Britain.

One of Burcot's residents, Rae Fowler, has collected these stories from
local people.

She points out that they have all been told to her by people who have
experienced the ghosts!!

During the Second World War, a bomb dropped on the village and
destroyed one of the cottages known as Dale Cottages. A lady living
there was killed. More recently, the cottages have been converted into
one house. The present owner woke up one morning and found a lady
leaning over her, who disappeared as she sat up. The people who live
in the house that was next to Dale Cottage (a house has recently been
built between them) have seen the lady several times. She has appeared to the father twice, the last appearance being this last Monday.
She always appears hanging over the person as he wakes up in bed in
the morning. Was it the ghost of the lady killed during the war?

Another incident occurred at one of the houses at Hewell Grange. A
lady moving into her new house smelt a strong smell of antiseptic.
This smell persisted for three days and she was later told that her
house had been built over the spot where a nurse had been murdered during the war.

At The Old House at the junction of Greenhill and Alcester Road,
the present owners were just moving in and as they passed an open
door they glanced into a room and saw a little girl dressed in Victorian costume. Being very busy and perhaps thinking it was a village
child in dressing-up clothes, they thought nothing of it until they met
people who lived at The Old House some years ago. During their conversation they asked if they had seen the little girl yet and apparently
the previous owners saw her several times, but she only shows herself
to females!

On the ground where the present County Gardens is built, there used
to be an old barn which apparently burned down one night and a body
of a tramp was found in the rubble next day. Some years later when
some greenhouses were erected, a workman took his little girl to work
with him. He left her to play and she came running back very excited
saying that she had seen 'a dirty old tramp walk straight through the
glass'.

Another story purports that the name of Vigo, covering the properties at the top end of the village beyond the sandstone railway bridge,
was bestowed on this group of ancient dwellings by the man who
built them. Legend has it that he was an old sea captain who made his

fortune plundering the treasure ships sailing in and out of the Spanish port of Vigo and it is said that on windy nights you can hear the sound of his ship's bell faintly in the distance. In support of the origin of Vigo, there is no doubt that the timbers in these old houses are certainly old ships' timbers probably dating back to pre-Armada days (pre 1588).

Rock - A funny man

About two miles to the north of Burcot, is the village of Rock. It lies at the foot of the Lickey Hills and Rock itself is 600 feet (183 metres) above sea level at its highest point. The Lickey hills are made up of five different types of rock, the youngest is 225 million years and the oldest is 570 million years! A doting aunt tells the story of this little girl in Rock.

My niece is only two years old. Her daddy was talking to his mother on the phone when the little girl kept shouting, 'Daddy, daddy'. He said to his mother, 'I'll have to call you back'.

He asked his daughter what was the matter. She said, 'Funny man'. Her daddy asked, 'Where's the man?' She said, 'Gone upstairs'. She clambered up a few stairs and looking up the stairs, said again, 'Daddy, funny man'. Then she added, 'Tick tock, tick tock'. A second or two later she said, 'Oh, funny man gone'.

I heard that quite often, the previous occupants saw the apparition of an unwashed old man who lived there on his own at the beginning of the 1900s. Sometimes they could smell him and they would call out, 'It's alright Joe' and the smell would disappear.

FECKENHAM - The gentleman vanishes

This is an enchanting village which, despite lying on the B4090 saltway only 4 km (2.5 miles) from the Redditch outskirts, has managed to escape redevelopment. The High Street has timber-framed house from most periods, together with several brick houses dating from the 1700s. It still has a little village green.

The old field names reveal a Feckenham haunted by spirits, ghosts and fairies. On the Tithe Award map of 1841 are two fields known respectively as Upper and Lower Puck Close, while to the north east was a field known as 'Sperrity pit'. About a mile to the north east is a medieval moated farmhouse known as Astwood Court occupied by generations of Culpeppers. The first Culpepper was an astrologer, a magician and a herbalist, said to have the ability to conjure up 'spirits of the planets', including a fierce tiger whose claws marked the table. In Feckenham Church is a memorial to the last of the Culpeppers who died in 1604 at the age of 25.

Feckenham was an administrative centre for the great forest of Fecken-ham which covered 60 villages and hamlets and was one of the favourite hunting grounds of early medieval kings. King John had a hunting lodge here and a depression in the ground near the church is all that is left of the court house which implemented the strict forest laws. In the 19th and 20th centuries it became heavily involved in needle-making.

Perhaps Margaret saw one of these needle makers . She was about thirty years of age when:

In the mid 1920s or it might even be as late as the early 1930s, my sister and I decided to go on a bicycle ride from Redditch town centre where we lived (the new town hadn't been built then) to Feckenham. It was a lovely ride in the summer, all country lanes. We were nearing Feckenham, cycling along Swansbrook Lane, and we were approach-ing the bridge that goes over Bow Brook when we saw a man standing on the bridge. He was wearing old-fashioned clothes, I would say, later than Victorian, more Edwardian, with a bowler hat and a jacket with a small collar. As I got closer – pop! – he suddenly disappeared. My sister and I looked at each other and said, 'Where's he gone?'.

That's been with me all these years. Where did he go?

ELCOCKS BROOK and strange goings-on at the Brook Inn!

About 3 km (2 miles) north of Feckenham is the hamlet of Elcocks Brook. Almost the only building here is the Brook Inn, the annex of which is 600 years old. The Brook Inn featured in *Ghosts Murders and Scandals of Worcestershire* published in 2005, when cups were smashed, articles disappeared,

The Brook Inn at Elcocks Brook.

a bell hanging over the bar rang of its own accord, and various mysterious shadows were seen by the staff.

A new member of staff arrived, Melinda, who discovered there was something strange about the pub on her very first day:

The Brook Inn is haunted, of course. I started working there about eleven months ago. On my first day, I had just set up the bar ready to open when I looked across the room and saw a bloke sitting there. My first thought was, 'How did he get in?' and then I thought, 'What strange clothes he has on'. He was wearing a tweed suit with a starched collar. The next second he had gone. I thought, 'I'm going mad'. Then the other staff told me that the place was haunted.

I have seen him several times. I've also seen a lady standing by the fireplace quite often. She's grey and white from head to toe and dressed in long white layers. She always looks very unhappy.

There are always goings-on at The Brook. We have a naughty ghost. It turns the lights on and off and stops the beer. Behind the bar are fridges for the drinks and at the bottom of each fridge is an on/off switch. You switch them on, turn round for a minute and when you turn back they're all off. Then you put something down and the next minute it's gone. It turns up somewhere else and you think, 'I'm sure I didn't put it there'.

Melinda has now gone to work in Spain.

TARDEBIGGE
Ghosts and scandals of Hewell Grange

If you look westward as you're driving along the Bromsgrove Highway between Redditch and Bromsgrove, you will see the spire of Tardebigge church. This is especially visible at night when it's illuminated. Nearby is the entrance to Hewell Grange, once the home of Lord Windsor whose descendents became the Earls of Plymouth. The Grange is now HM Youth Custody Centre and two prisons have been built in its grounds. The story of how Lord Windsor came to be living here is almost unbelievable.

It goes back to the time of Henry VIII. In the 1530s the king closed all the abbeys and monasteries and appropriated their wealth, including Bordesley Abbey in Redditch. The wily old abbot of Bordesley, who pretended to be senile, had already disposed of its assets so that all that Henry VIII got in 1538 was an estate worth seventy shillings and a debt of £200, plus the land.

Henry VIII decided that the best way to recoup his interests was to swap it for a more lavish building. Four years later he went to dine with Lord Windsor in his splendid castle at Stanwell in Middlesex. Lord Windsor was appalled when he later received instructions that he was to hand Stanwell over to the king and move out immediately to Bordesley Abbey. His castle was stocked with Christmas provisions and he had to leave them behind. The story goes that he arrived on a cold wet November afternoon with his retinue to find the abbey inhabitable. He decided to move into Hewell grange, a farmhouse at Tardebigge belonging to the abbey.

Hewell Grange has been rebuilt several times. For many years the ruins of an old house and the new one stood together in the grounds but when the Shah of Persia visited in 1889 the old house was blown up for entertainment.

The grounds were landscaped and included a large lake. From time to time a white lady has been seen drifting across the water. The late Arthur Bunnegar always maintained that, just before the Grange became a prison, he was chestnutting in the grounds late one chilly November afternoon with half-a-dozen of his friends when they saw a lady rise slowly from the lake. She was wearing a huge white voluminous dress 'like a ballroom gown' and as she walked towards the derelict ballroom her dress flowed and fluttered.

In about 1819, Hewell Grange was inherited by Lady Harriet, a conscientious Christian land-owner who did her best to bring her properties up to a

Hewell Grange at its height.

55

high standard. She worshipped in Tardebigge Church every Sunday. Opposite the church was the Magpie Inn and the story goes that the vicar would set his congregation working their way through the singing of the psalms while he nipped across to the Magpie for a quick pint. Lady Harriet hated the Magpie so much that she removed the pub sign.

The ground drops sharply by the side of the church to the Birmingham and Worcester canal, a nightmare for boats and barges as the longest flight of navigable locks is here, with 30 locks climbing 217 feet (66m)! Nearby is the start of the 580 yard (634 metres) Tardebigge tunnel where boats had to be taken through by 'leggers', ie a men lying in his back on the boat and 'walking' along the walls. The leggers used to wait for work in The Magpie with the result that some of them began work after they had had far too much to drink. When one of them fell into the canal and was drowned, Lady Harriet closed the inn, added a new frontage and turned it into a school. New school buildings were added later and the original school (which had been the Magpie Inn) became a house for the caretaker and his family.

A poltergeist goes to school

Michelle moved into the school house in about 1993 with her two daughters, the eldest would have been about nine years of age and the youngest three. She says:

All kinds of things happened while we were there.

Several times the landing light bulb shot out of its socket and hit a wall but it wasn't broken. We would just collect it and screw it back in. Another time the light bulb descended from its fitting, went across the room and set itself down very slowly.

In an old cupboard I found some pictures, some stamps and a crucifix. I hung the crucifix on the stairs. Every morning I would come down and the crucifix would be upside down, and there would be a spot of blood underneath it on the wall. I kept wiping it off and the next morning the spot would be back again. In the end I put the crucifix back in the cupboard

My daughter (who was nine-ish) was sitting in the kitchen having her tea, when suddenly she screamed. Something had smacked her on the face. I had a look at her and on her face was the mark of an adult hand. She said she hadn't screamed from the slap but because, when she looked up, nobody was there.

One night, my daughter came into my bedroom and woke me up and she and I spent the night hiding under the bed. We could hear whistling and singing, and a curious rolling noise, then there would be a thud, then the rolling noise would stop for a few minutes, then the noise would start again. It could possibly have been the sound of barrels being dropped down the cellar. I'm a firm believer in the 'Stone-Tape' theory where past events impregnate themselves into the brickwork and some individuals can pick them up in later years.

I had a very vivid dream one night. On my right-hand side I could see pale wisps of smoke and then I saw a flash of red. A policewoman was there, her name was Jane and I could see the number on her tunic so clearly that, when I woke up in the morning, I wrote it down.

About two weeks later I stayed over at work for half an hour or so, it was probably about halfpast five or a quarter to six when I was driving up the approach to our house. From behind the church I saw the same, pale, wispy smoke that I had seen in my dream. My father and I called the fire brigade and I stood at the bottom of the drive to direct the fire engine in the right direction. As it went past, I realised that it was the flash of red I had seen in my dream. Some teenagers had been playing in the churchyard and had lit a fire in front of the boiler house which was taking hold. The firemen said that in another half-an-hour, it would have reached the oil-fired boiler and there would have been a tremendous explosion.

A policewoman was investigating, her name was Jane and she had the same number that I had seen in my dream. I told the constable and she thought I had gone mad, so I showed her the number that I had

The School House at Tardebigge. It was originally a a public house, the Mapie, then Tardebigge School, and finally residential accommodation.

written down. Then she suspected me of arson!

Curious things often happened when we had visitors, I felt it was done for effect as we never reacted and the visitors would react. For example, the windows had shutters but they were fixed against the all, so we freed them, but they were very stiff, it needed some effort to move them. Once, when we had visitors, the shutters opened and closed rapidly several times. There was no way you could have moved them yourself as quickly as that.

Eventually we called the vicar in and he organised somebody to come from Worcester to bless the property. But it didn't help.

I never felt scared, the house had a nice, homely atmosphere. Sometimes I did feel annoyed. I left some money on the kitchen table one morning, I went out of the room to fetch my handbag and when I returned the money had gone. We never found it. I was the only one in the house. I was annoyed then, I said, 'Oh do stop it' and things did go quiet for a little while, but they came back eventually. I felt as if I was sharing the house with someone I couldn't see, but it was not at all scary. In fact, sometimes it was quite a comfortable feeling, you were never lonely.

When we left the house the property was renovated. My mother happened to be assisting at the school at that time and she heard that the builders were having problems. Their tools were going missing and one evening, they left the skirting boards out all ready to be fitted and when they returned the next morning the boards had all been piled up in the middle of the room.

The scandal of the village hall

Following heavy death duties the Plymouth estate was sold in 1946.

A scandal arose which the villagers still regard with bitterness. Lord Plymouth built a fantastic village hall for Tardebigge folk, it even had a row of cookers for the young ladies to have cookery lessons. The hall belonged to the villagers and should not have been sold. The tale is told that the deeds could not be found so the villagers could not prove that the hall belonged to them. Even worse, the auctioneers sold a parcel of land without realising that the village hall was included, consequently it was sold at minimal cost and bought by a local consortium. They refused to return it to the villagers for the price they paid for it.

The village hall became the public house, the Tardebigge. In about 1991, the staff asked a local medium to visit as so many strange things were happening. Two-pint tankards suddenly split down the middle, the barman was

The Tardebigge, now a public house but originally a village hall.

scared out of his wits when someone sneezed behind him in the cellar, a dastardly laugh was heard by the cleaner, staff heard their names called and were frequently tapped on the shoulder. The medium suggested that it was haunted by a nurse from the First World War.

The hounds of Grampound

One of the stalls in the Bromsgrove market hall is held by a retired gentleman who goes under the name of 'Panda'. He told the following story:

Late one night a few years ago, I was driving from St Austel to Penzance in a hired wagon, helping a lady friend of mine to move house to Penzance. I was driving through Grampound when suddenly I saw two big dogs running along the road straight towards me. They must have been Great Danes to be that size. There was no chance of stopping in time and both of them went straight into the front of the car.

I stopped the car and we had a look round but couldn't see anything. I thought, 'Those poor dogs, I have hit them'. It was late evening and I was anxious to unload, so I drove on. We unloaded in Penzance and I stayed the night. The next morning, as soon as it was light, I went back expecting to see two dead dogs in the road but there was nothing. I asked several people round about if they had seen two

59

large dogs running about, possibly injured, or if anyone locally had two large dogs but I drew a blank. I can see them in my mind's eye today. They were so clear.

A slip in time

Most of us have heard of time slips, to but to meet somebody who has actually experienced one is very rare. Kate, who lives in Bromsgrove, told us of a visit to the Edinburgh Festival in summer during the mid 1970's when, while walking around the Grass Market, close to the Church of St. John's, near Princess Street, she found herself in an open Square with everyone dressed in 16th century clothing.

I kept to the shady side of the Square, enjoying the sunshine and tranquillity of the afternoon, when suddenly, without any warning, I was surrounded by many people milling around, going about their business, with one significant exception, they were all dressed in clothing that seemed more in keeping with the 16th Century than the 21st.

In front of me stood two people - a man and a woman, with their backs to me. He was sturdy in appearance, wearing a blue jacket and drab coloured breeches, white stockings, white shirt, and a flattish black pill-box type hat made of soft material. The woman was slim and wore a rather dull brown dress, with a white collar and a bonnet. I stood watching, enthralled by what was happening without any fear whatsoever, noticing the man seemed rather excited about something because he kept waving his arms about. Unfortunately, I was unable to make out the conversation, or accent, because of the noise emanating from the surrounding crowd. Suddenly, without warning, 'almost like a slide being withdrawn from a projector', the whole scenario in front of me began to fizzle out and fade away before returning to the normality of the previous afternoon.

I do not believe that my experience could be explained away as an illusion, mirage, or the product of an over-active imagination. I firmly believe, for reasons beyond my understanding, I was taken back into time for a short period and that those events were very real.

6. CLENT AND ROMSLEY AREA

 early nine hundred years ago, in about 1113, one of the monks or scribes working in the cloisters of Worcester cathedral, began an impressive new project. Florence of Worcester started work on a history of England. After five years of concentrated labour he died, but the history was continued by another monk. The work is now of great importance. Florence's reference books were, of course, very limited with the result that some of his accounts of past events are inaccurate. Such an event is the murder of St Kenelm. However, the story caught the imagination of the early church, so that we have at least ten churches dedicated either to Saint Kenelm or to Our Lady and Saint Kenelm. The village of Kenelmstow developed around the spot where the young prince's body is thought to have been found. 'Stow' means a place of importance, and it became a major centre for pilgrims seeking forgiveness of sins and healing of ailments. Of course, they paid for the privilege.

A summary for those not familiar with the legend is as follows: On the death of the Mercian king Kenulph in 819, his young son Kenelm became king at the age of seven. However, his older sister Quendryh had her eye on the throne and, planned to murder the young king with the help of his foster father, Askebert. First they tried to poison him, and when that failed, they decided that Askebert would take him hunting in the Clent Hills where Kenelm would meet with 'an accident'. The night before he was murdered, Kenelm had a dream in which he climbed a large decorated tree from where he could see the four quarters of his kingdom. Three of the quarters bowed down to him but the fourth chopped the tree down. Kenelm then flew away as a white bird. When the young prince related his dream to his wise old nurse, she wept, as she realised that he was to die.

Askbert went off with Kenelm to the Clent Hills. The young prince faced death bravely but he was beheaded and his body hidden under a thorn tree. His spirit flew as a white dove to the Pope with the message 'Low in a mead of kind under a thorn, of head bereft, lieth poor Kenelm king-born'. Consequently, the Pope wrote to the Archbishop of Canterbury asking him to find the body, and a party was sent out from Winchcombe. They were guided to the spot by various signs including a shaft of light. When the body was taken up, a spring gushed from the spot. He was taken to Winchester for burial.

Winchcombe Abbey once stood to the east of St Peter's Church in Winchcombe. When the sad funeral procession reached the city, bells rang of their own accord. Quenryda asked what this meant and was told that her brother had been murdered and his body had been brought to the abbey. She was reading a psalter and said, 'If that be true, may both my eyes fall upon this psalter'. With that, both her eyes dropped out and fell on the book.

The psalter, with its bloodstains running down the pages, was a prized possession of Winchcombe Abbey until it was stolen a few years ago. Quenryda and Askebert were killed and their bodies thrown into a ditch.

Miracles began to occur at St Kenelm's shrine at Winchombe, providing another lucrative attraction for pilgrims.

As for the truth of the legend, there was a King Kenelm but unfortunately he came to the throne when he was 12, not seven. He probably died in 811 when he was 25 years old and his sister was not the wicked murderer but a hallowed nun who became an Abbess.

As for the spring, the present site, attractive though it may be, is not the original one.

The original spring could have been in a field to the north of the church, full of bumps and hollows. The old village of Kenelmstowe was situated here. The enclosure is surrounded by a bank, and in the corner are the remains of an old sandstone building. Behind the building is a small pool, surrounded by bushes and trees. There's a possibility that this may have been the original well. In 1735, Bishop Charles Lyttelton wrote a history of Hagley in which he said that Kenelmstowe had disappeared but the well was still there, 'handsomely coped with stone and much resorted to both before and since the Reformation by the superstitious vulgar for the cure of sore eyes and other maladies'.

The learned architect, Sir Nikolaus Pevsner, suggests an alternative site. He says that the church was built to protect the well. Below the east end of the church is an undercoft containing the holy spring and the blocked arch in the south wall of the chancel led to the stairway down.

(Some of this information came from the Romsley and Hunnington Society website)

BELBROUGHTON – Transported at fifteen!

Situated on the lower slopes of the Clent Hills between Bromsgrove and Kidderminster, Belbroughton is a surprisingly attractive village. By the time William the Conqueror compiled the 1086 Domesday Book, a priest was living here in a little Saxon Church. Holy Trinity Church now stands on the same spot and although it has been rebuilt many times, fragments go as far back as the 13th century.

For about 400 years Belbroughton was famous for its agricultural tools such as scythes, hay knives and chaff knives.

In 1787, a fifteen year old servant girl in Belboughton, Sarah Bellamy, was accused of stealing. She was transported to Australia on the First Fleet. There is, however, a happy ending to this story, two hundred years later the anniversary of the First Fleet was celebrated in Portsmouth and two of Sarah's great, great, great, grand-daughters arrived from Sydney. They visited Belbroughton and a plaque on the village green commemorates their visit.

The population has grown during the last fifty years with many new houses but there are still plenty of old houses and picturesque cottages such as the one featured in the next narrative, told by the young man's mother:

The odd slippers

My son's girlfriend moved from Bromsgrove to a cottage in Belbroughton. She had trouble from the first day they moved in. She felt that someone was watching her. The television would switch itself on and off and the lights would go and off. She was quite concerned and called in an electrician out but he couldn't find anything wrong.

A neighbour told her that a grandmother had lived there previously with her two grandchildren and she had died suddenly. The girlfriend had two children – whether or not the old lady had come back, attracted by the two children, I don't know.

Anyhow, my son decided to clear the loft. Up in the loft were two empty suitcases with labels on them saying 'Switzerland' and various countries, belonging to the previous owner of the house. He brought

The pretty little village of Belbroughton.

them down and, before taking them to the tip, he put them in an empty cupboard downstairs in the entrance hall. After that, his girlfriend would shut the cupboard doors each night but every morning they would be open.

He thought perhaps this was something to do with the suitcases so on the way to his home, he took them to the tip. His girlfriend put the children to bed.

The next day, at work , he got a call from his girlfriend. Without doubt the cupboard had been empty but the next morning she found the cupboard doors open and when she looked in the cupboard two slippers were there, one pink and one blue. She mentioned it to a neighbour who told her that the old lady often wore a pair of slippers, one pink and one blue.

Things have died down now but they still have peculiar things happening. If they put the TV on it changes channels all by itself. They're not bothered. They think it's just the old lady objecting to the programme they're watching.

BLAKEDOWN – The floating pint

Blakedown is three miles from Kidderminster and on the green belt. Since 1777 the village has been cut in two by a highway, first the turnpike road, then the main Kidderminster to Birmingham trunk road. The village grew rapidly when the Oxford, Worcester and Wolverhampton railway arrived, known as the Old Worse and Worse because of its unreliable rolling stock.

Blakedown has a lively community and one of its societies is The Churchill and Blakedown '41' Club. At a meeting on 4 November 2008, the Chairman told the following story about his holiday at the Niedd Warner Leisure Hotel in Harrogate, a beautiful Georgian building set in 45 acres of garden.

About two years ago I was staying in a Warner Hotel at Niedd Hall in Yorkshire. They had put on a cabaret in the evening and we were inside the bar having a drink. I sat down with a pint of beer, full up to the top. I took a few sips and put it back on the table. It rose in the air several inches, came towards me and tipped right upside down. It went everywhere. I had to go and change. It was as if someone came up from underneath the pint and slowly and deliberately tipped it in my lap.

Someone asked if it was on the edge of the table. No, it was right in the middle.

The night porter said that sort of thing had happened before.

7. DROITWICH AND WYCHBOLD

roitwich is, of course, famous for its 'white gold'. Droit-wich was once the chief supplier of salt across the whole of England. It sits on a huge saltwater lake where the brine is highly concentrated, 4.5 litres (1 gallon) of brine produces about 1.32 kilogrms (2.9 lb) of salt. The traditional method of producing the salt is simply to boil it, then collect the wet crystals and place them in another container to drain and form a block.

Fortunes have been made and lost at Droitwich. The wells were heavily regulated and no-one else was allowed to bore a pit, but in 1670 Robert Steynor bored two salt pits on his own land. The case went to court and he won, but he was ruined by the costs. After that, everyone was boring pits and the price of salt dropped, ruining many people who had invested in salt, including some schools and hospitals.

The industry was at its height in 1872, when 120,000 tons of salt were produced.

Two thousand years ago, someone in Droitwich committed a murder and did his best to cover it up. No-one knows the identity of the either the murderer or the murdered. The Romans settled in Droitwich and in about the second century, they closed one of the salt wells and filled it in with rubbish. When the well was recently investigated, archaeologists discovered, in with the rubble, the skeleton of a fifteen year old boy or girl. In his booklet *Savouring the Past*, JD Hurst remarks that this is 'suggestive of some terrible deed being covered up'.

More than fourteen other skeletons were found in 1980 on the northeast side of Vines Lane, between Bays Meadow Villa and Dodderhill Fort, but these were from a Roman cemetery.

Gossip from the Heritage and Tourist Information Centre

The Heritage and Tourist Information Centre is in a 1930s black and white building which stands on the site of one of Richard Corbett's brine baths of 1880. When a young man, Corbett was given a small sum of money by his parents with which he bought a run-down salt mine at Stoke Prior. Using the latest extraction methods, he managed to produce exceptionally pure salt with the result that Stoke Prior became a major salt supplier. Corbett became rich beyond his wildest dreams, he was known as 'The Salt King' and he built the Chateau Impney. He then turned his attention to Droitwich

and developed the town as a spa.

The Heritage Centre holds exhibitions and arranges workshops and lectures. In July 2007 the TIC was staffed by two volunteers, Judy and Ann, who told us:

We hear lots of gossip about ghosts in Droitwich. It's such a very old town. There was an electrical place in the High Street and people said that as they walked up the stairs they got a very strange feeling. In Priory House, the people who worked there said all kinds of peculiar things happened. They would put down a pencil or a biro and it would disappear straight away. A cavalier has been seen several times on the Chawson estate, and they say that a white horse and rider have been seen on the bridge over Copcut Lane when it's misty. There's said to be a tunnel from Dodderhill churchyard to Priory House, the railway cut straight across it. It's said to be linked with the Saltway. Once every 50 years a headless cavalier is supposed to ride through the tunnel and emerge.

Murder at Priory House

The staff at the Tourist Information Office have mentioned Priory House, this is the beautiful Elizabethan dwelling at the cul-de-sac end of Friar Street.

There's an old legend about the house. At one time, it belonged to the Carbury family, all members of which had died out except for two cousins, Sir Richard Carbury and Lucretia. It was decided that, to perpetuate the line, the two should marry, the only difficulty being that they couldn't stand the sight of each other.

Far left: Saint Richard's house, Tourist Informa-tion Centre. Near Left: Priory House, Friar Street.

Sir Richard said that he wasn't bothered about his inheritance and in 1738 went to America and joined a regiment. After about ten years, he decided that perhaps his inheritance wasn't such a bad thing after all, so he returned to Droitwich and, one evening, knocked at the door of the house. Lucretia welcomed him with open arms, fed him well, saw that he was comfortably settled in a back bedroom then, in the middle of the night, stabbed him to death.

The story goes that he was buried in the garden which once stretched across to Vines Park. His body is supposedly preserved by the brine in the salt springs. If you are driving on the Saltway past Vines Park and cold shivers go up your spine, you may have run over the body of Sir Richard Carbury.

Sir Richard is supposed to appear every 50 years. He was seen on April 14 1875 by Mrs Porter, who was staying temporarily at the house. She was the matron of a boy's school but as she was suffering from rheumatics, she had been sent to Droitwich to visit the brine baths. At that time, Priory House had a grand staircase lined with family portraits, including one of Sir Richard and another of Lucretia.

Mrs Porter described her experience in a letter to her cousin. As the church clock at St Andrew's struck twelve, she saw a tall, ghostly figure at the bottom of her bed. It was Sir Richard, and he spent the next hour detailing his life story and his murder.

Evidently Sir Richard is not very good at mathematics as he did not appear again until about 68 years later and then in a monk's garb. A

67

descendent of the young lady who saw the ghost now lives in Evesham and says:

My aunty would have been 86 by now. When she was about 18 or 20 she worked as a maid at Priory House. She was sleeping in a room there with her sister, Iris, when she woke up and saw a monk sitting on the edge of their bed. My aunty blinked, and when she opened her eyes, the monk had gone.

Unfortunately, Nellie Copson, the local historian, says that there is no truth in the tale and the house was owned by the Norbury family, not the Carbury. However, could Mrs Porter have misremembered or misread the name on the painting?

A Roman ghost helps in the stock-taking

Nearly every collection of Worcestershire ghost stories contains a sighting of a Roman; in this book we have one in the Evesham chapter. Perhaps the best Droitwich anecdote comes from *Unquiet Spirits of Worcestershire* published in 1999 and it's such a good story we're repeating it here. Robert Nicklin worked at a company on the Berryhill Estate, Droitwich, for ten years, from 1987 to 1997.

The Roman in the factory. He walked straight through the machines! An imaginative reconstruction, Roman supplied by Discover History at discover-history.co.uk.

When I first started, we used to do a stock-take twice a year which would take the whole day and the factory would be closed. Normally the factory is very noisy but for the stock-take, the machines would all be turned off and the dead silence would be very creepy.

We were still working at about nine-thirty or ten pm one night. There were just the three of us, Nick Williams, myself and a third person in the office. Nick and I were sent to the other end of the factory to do a recheck. We were walking up the factory when we both saw what I swear was a Roman soldier. It was very dark so I could only see a dark shape, but I could make out his shield, which was rectangular, about four feet long and two-and-a-half feet wide, and his helmet, which was a bit like a World War I German soldier's helmet with a point on top and a crest. I was sideways on to him and Nick was coming up from behind. This Roman soldier was walking in a straight line, and you can't do that in a factory, the machines are in the way, so he was walking through the machines. I couldn't believe what I saw and thought someone must be playing a joke on us, so I said to my mate, 'You go round that way and I'll go round this. If somebody's still here, messing us about, we want to know who it is'.

We came together and it was obvious nobody was about. I looked at Nick and he looked at me and he said, 'Let's go'. I said, 'I'm not stopping here, I'm off down the office'.

I haven't seen anything before or since. We often meet up and we have a laugh over it. Nobody has been able to explain it. Somebody did tell me that there's an old Roman burial ground under the Berryhill estate.

The Case of the Sexy Slimmer

A Droitwich couple were involved in a famous murder in 1977, known as 'The Case of the Sexy Slimmer'. Barbara Cooper was one of the first women in England to have an operation to help her reduce weight. Her weight went from 23 stone to 15 and she became very sexy.

Her husband, George, was 37 years of age and a marketing manager. A neighbour, John, knew George well and says:

I lived in a mid-terraced house in Woodman's Close on the Westlands Estate for four years. One day my neighbour, George Cooper, from two doors up came to see me to ask if I had seen his wife about because she had gone missing. He told me how he had been to see the doctor because he was tired all day and had blurred vision.

It turned out that his wife had been making him a late-night drink and lacing it with sleeping pills so that she could slip out and meet her lover, Mervyn Collins, a fork lift driver from where she worked. They had gone off together to a house near Wakefield in West Yorkshire.

A few days later George traced her from a credit card invoice and went up there taking with him a shotgun Barbara had bought him for his birthday.

Dwarfing the trees, the Wychbold radio masts.

At Leeds Crown Court, George stated that he went up there to try and get her back. When Mervyn came to the door, George confronted him. Mervyn grinned and said, 'You're the one who couldn't manage your wife, not me'. George lost his temper and the gun went off twice. He said that he had no intention of hurting anyone. Barbara survived a shot to her belly but Mervyn was killed by a second shot.

The Judge said that George's life had been one of patience and under-standing. He had stood by his wife although she became grotesque when she had ballooned to 23 stone. He had nursed her and looked after her. The defending QC said that he was still deeply in love with his wife and filled with remorse. George was sentenced to six years.

The law did not allow the wife to be called as a witness, so she sat outside the courtroom with their twelve-year old son.

WYCHBOLD - Ghosts and Spies

A young lady from Wychbold went on holiday to Germany. When she was asked where she lived, she said shyly, 'Oh, you won't know it, it's a tiny vil-lage in Worcestershire, Wychbold'. 'Wychbold!' exclaimed her hosts, 'Of course we know it. We used to listen to the broadcasts from there during the war. It was the only way we could get reliable information'.

The Wychbold transmitters are a well-known landmark and can be seen for miles around. They were established in 1934 and are still the BBC's most powerful longwave transmitters. The Radio 4 LW signal from Droitwich is the strongest in the UK. The two highest masts are 700 feet (210m) high.

The Droitwich transmitter helped England to win the war. There were only a few transmitters in England capable of broadcasting to radios right across Europe. It was used to send secret messages in code to the French resist-ance and it played a part in the D-Day landings on 6 June 1944. The date of the landings was broadcast in code as part of a poem. The day before, messages were sent out to the resistance to carry out acts of sabotage.

However, the Germans were listening into the messages right through the war and their code breakers were desperately trying to unravel the secret messages. They even managed to use the apparatus themselves and send their own messages from the transmitter!

After the D-Day landings, photographs of Droitwich transmitting station were found in an airfield behind enemy lines. They were taken not from the air, but from the ground. There must have been a spy in the area. No-one has any idea who this could have been.

The airfield even has a ghost. At the Bromsgrove Antique Collector's Fair of 26 November 2008, an elderly lady told this story. She's 95% certain that the local station was Wychbold but there's a remote possibility it could have been Gaydon.

My husband was a wireless operator and he saw a ghost at the local station after the war, in the early 1950s. Anyhow, he was coming back after a night on. It was early morning, he was tired and a mist had spread. As he was walking across he came round a corner and he could see a man all dressed up like a rigger. The man went into an old building. My husband thought, 'He's on his shift early, but that's good, there will be somebody to walk back with', so he waited, but nobody came out of the building. Then he bumped into another of the riggers. He said, 'I've just seen one of your riggers going into the old building. I waited for him to come out but he never came'. The second rigger said, 'Take no notice, he's always coming back. He always said he was going to die in his bed and where the dining room is now was where the beds were'.

8. THE EVESHAM AREA

n Evesham market place is a statue of a man sheltering under trees with pigs roaming at his feet. The work is by the sculptor, John McKenna; it was unveiled in June 2008 and financed by local people. Its purpose is to commemorate the charming story of the founding of Evesham Abbey, The plinth on which it stands is made from stone from the original Abbey and donated by readers of the Cotswold and Vale Magazine.

The old legend of the foundation of Evesham is well known. To summarise, a humble swineherd, Eoves, was minding his pigs one day on the banks of the river Avon when he wandered into an area he had not seen before. There he saw a vision of three angels, the centre angel being more beautiful and taller than the others. Eoves rushed to tell Egwin, the Bishop of Worcester, remembered as Saint Egwin. The bishop had just returned from a visit to the Pope as his preaching, particularly against working on a Sunday and adultery, had made him unpopular in some quarters and there were those who wanted him removed from his post. The story goes that Egwin chained his feet together, fastened the chains with a lock and threw away the key into the Avon before setting out. While he was at Rome, a salmon was caught in the Tiber and when it was cooked by his attendants, the key was found inside the fish. This 'miracle' so impressed the Pope that Egwin was sent home in honour.

The bishop promised God that if he retained his post he would found a monastery, and here was the perfect place. The story goes that the bishop knelt and had the same vision but this time the central angel reached out and touched him, showing that she was the Virgin Mary. The building of his great monastery began in about 714.

Statue in Evesham of the swineherd's vision

The scandalous Duke Alphere

By the time Egwin died in about AD717, the monastery was rich and famous. In about 976 Duke Alphere, Prince of the great kingdom of Mercia, acquired the monasteries. He turned the monks out, stripped them of their treasures and reduced them to poverty. Divine retribution came and he fell sick. Thinking that he had not long to live, he sent for one of the monks, gave him back everything he had stolen and asked him to be abbot and take charge of the monastery. However, the canons refused to leave and so the abbot swapped the monastery for one in Towcester. The Duke of Alphere is said to have died in miserable circumstances, alone and 'eaten by vermin'.

Another villain who stripped the monastery of its riches was, surprisingly, its abbot, Roger Norreys who was appointed during the reign of Richard I in 1191. He lived a life of luxury while the monks were in such a poor state that they could not preach as they 'had no breeches' and they had to beg for food. He ruled for an incredible 22 years and was finally deposed in 1213.

A Roman surprise

Six centuries or so before Egwin founded his monastery, the Romans were in Evesham. Properly, they should be described as Romano-British as the ancient Brits soon realized that the continental way of life was superior and joined forces. Various pieces of Roman pottery have been found but there had been no concrete evidence of their existence.

Then, in 1996, property at numbers 95 to 97 High Street were to be pulled down and the developers financed an archaeological dig. The finds were so important that English Heritage gave more financial support for the dig to continue. In addition to Iron Age features were Roman field boundaries, confirming the existence of Romans in Evesham. One archaeologist remarked that it was a surprise, 'Evesham is not a town one associates with the Romans'.

Equally surprised, if not more so, was a young lady returning from a shopping expedition:

One late summer night in 1990, a friend and I had been shopping in Cheltenham and upon arriving back in Evesham decided to go into Evesham town centre to get something to eat. As we were driving down Abbey Road I suddenly found my eyes drawn to what appeared to be a centuria of Romans marching down the road. I told my friend to look out the car window and just see if she could see anything. She just sat there with her mouth opening and closing and then one word came out 'Romans'!

By this time I had slowed right down to about 5mph and we drew up next to them. We could only see about five-and-a-half men across as they disappeared into the telephone exchange but there were 10 rows of them. They also appeared to have lost their bodies below

74

their knees - I would imagine that this was because the road in Roman times was much higher than in the 20th century. They appeared to turn and then completely disappeared. Although this happened almost 20 years ago I still look out for Romans whenever I travel down Abbey Road!

The Battle of Evesham and its shadows.

Evesham is famous for the great battle of 1265 between Simon de Montfort and the royalists under Prince Edward, who later became Edward I. De Montfort represented the barons, who believed that the king was too powerful. Evesham, of course, is bounded on three sides by the river Avon. While De Montfort waited for reinforcements, he camped with his army in the loop of the river believing he was safe, but he was trapped. In pouring rain, the king's forces, led by Prince Edward, came streaming down Greenhill. Some Chroniclers reckon that 160 knights and 4,000 men of Simon's army were killed including his son, while Simon himself was hacked to pieces.

Simon's head and hands were placed in a bag which was sewn up and sent to Lady Mortimer at Wigmore as trophy. The messenger found her at mass at a nearby abbey. He entered the church just as the priest was elevating the host. The story goes that as he told Lady Mortimer the news, the hands of Earl Simon were seen to clasp themselves in prayer above the messenger's head, although they were afterwards found inside the bag. Lady Mortimer was so alarmed that she sent the hands back to Evesham. The monks of Evesham gathered any other remains and buried them in their church. Miracles soon began to be performed at the tomb. His remains are now buried in Abbey Park behind the two churches. As the years have passed, he has become a national hero for striking the first blow for democracy. Details of the battle are in the Almonry museum, including booklets and a model of the battlefield.

The narrator of the following story is anxious that his location should not be revealed, but we can say that he lives on the battlefield site:

An old document describes the battle of Evesham.

These things happened during the first few weeks that we moved in. We all used to see cloudy shadows of a man upstairs. Our little boy refused to go up. I saw a shadow out of the corner of my eye about twice a day for the first month, I would turn round to look at it but it had gone.

Someone came to the house who claimed that she could see him and even talk to him. She said it was an old man who lived there beforehand and all the changes made him unsettled. We were changing things round, painting the house, etcetera. After a month or so we sorted ourselves out, we finished making changes and it all died down. But we're planning to make a lot more changes to the house and we wonder if he'll appear again.

(We have several cases of alterations to a property producing a ghost.)

Ghosts in Boots

Bridge Street is the only bridge over the Avon on the eastern side of the town. Charles I stayed at a house in Bridge Street in 1644, during the civil wars. These were exciting times. Charles was trying to escape from the parliamentarians who were closing in on him, a process which was hampered by an enormous baggage train of supplies, armaments and thirty coaches of ladies with their belongings! Charles was eventually captured and beheaded in 1649.

Over the years several shops in Bridge Street have claimed to be haunted. Here is one of them:

For several years I worked in Boots the Chemist. I was very often upstairs on my own, packaging medication for the many nursing homes we supplied. One afternoon I was running a bit late and needed some items from downstairs. As I walked across the warehouse I saw one of the shop floor staff and so I called out to her (my reasoning was that she could get what I needed and pop it in the lift for me then I could pick it up later).

As she walked around the racking I called her again but she ignored me. I followed her and was about to tease her about having cloth ears when I saw her walk through a wall!

Just at this moment the warehouse door swung open and the lady in question walked in. I must have looked quite strangely at her and she asked what was up. I told her what I had seen and she looked quite shocked and surprised, then she confessed that she had seen something similar a few weeks before but had thought she was imagining it.

The lady was very slim and wearing a long navy skirt and a white blouse finely patterned with blue, her hair was in a bun and I saw her several times afterwards. She always seemed oblivious to my presence as she went about her daily business.

The phantom pantie-knicker

Wendy told this story at Evesham car Boot in July 2008, with interruptions from her husband, Mike:

In the summer of 2002 we went to stay at the Sun Inn at Hook Norton for a mid-week holiday. (Mike says that he went for the Hook Norton ales as much as anything). It was a lovely, friendly inn and we were made very welcome.

When we got there, they were hosting the biggest funeral I have ever seen. You can tell how many mourners there were, some of them had been brought by coach and it was full. The number of mourners showed clearly that he was a popular and well-loved guy. We were trying to have a happy holiday and everywhere you looked were mourners. It made for a very strange atmosphere. We went for a walk round the back next to the church and you could hear the shovels scraping in the graveyard.

We had a lovely four-poster bed but the room felt very odd. There was something not quite right about it. I couldn't sleep at night and we kept hearing plumbing noises, creaking and footsteps in the corridor coming towards our door, sometimes it sounded as if they were coming into our room.

In the morning when I went to get dressed I found that my bright red knickers had disappeared. I knew exactly where I had put them and they had gone. We searched everywhere but we never found them. We left a message at the reception desk in case they came to light after we had gone home and the room was cleaned, but no-one ever found them.

BADSEY - The old gent

In the heart of the Evesham Plain is the village of Badsey. One of its old buildings is Seyne House, originally a convalescent home for the 'sick and bloodied' monks of Evesham Abbey. When the Abbey was dissolved by HenryVIII the house was occupied by the Lord of the Manor. Unfortunately, the narrator of the next story is unable to remember the name and exact location of the property concerned but it was probably Seyne House.

About four years ago one of my neighbours asked me if I'd go with her to have a look at an old house in Badsey that they were thinking of buying. They thought it might need a lot of work and as we've done up a few houses she thought I'd have an idea of what might need doing and how much it would cost.

Anyway, we pulled up in front of the house and went inside. The house had a lovely feel about it, sort of homely and welcoming. We went inside and the estate agent told us to just wander around. I was drawn to the upstairs and went into this one large bedroom where I saw an old man sitting in a chair. I apologised for not knocking and went to leave him in peace. He told me not to be silly and it was nice to see someone. He then proceeded to tell me all about his garden and family. I was quite deep in conversation with him, thinking what a lovely old gent he was when my friend and the estate agent walked in and asked me who I was talking to. I gestured with my hand towards the gentleman and said 'this lovely gentleman here' except that I couldn't finish the word 'here' as I realised that the chair was empty! I was completely speechless and my friend couldn't get out of the house quickly enough!

This is a fairly common experience and one which is recorded in many collections of ghost stories. In *Strange Meetings* by the author and Barrie Roberts, a couple went to view a house in Coventry. The husband went to look upstairs and saw an 'old dear' coming down the staircase. He pressed himself against the newel post to let her go by and she went straight through him!

HONEYBOURNE – Riots and murders

Honeybourne and Pebworth are about 1.5 miles apart, (2 km) and lie in an arm of Worcestershire stretching out on the south east, with Warwickshire to the north and Gloucestershire to the south. Six hundred years ago, several Honeybourne folk were murdered by men from Evesham.

In early medieval times Honeybourne was divided into two, Honeybourne itself and Cow Honeybourne. The first was in Worcestershire, the latter in Gloucestershire and there was a church in both parts. The Worcestershire church was built in 1295 and dedicated to St Egwin. It belonged to Evesham Abbey who received its rich tithes and offerings. However, there was a controversy over who owned the Gloucestershire church. Evesham Abbey said it belonged to them as it was closely related to the Worcestershire church and the Prior of Winchcomb thought it should belong to him as it was in his county.

Eventually, the matter was settled by the Gloucestershire church being given to Evesham, while the Abbot of Winchcomb received compensation of money and property.

A condition of the agreement was that although the men of both Honeybourne churches could worship in their own church for normal services, for special services they were to take part in a grand procession to Evesham Abbey. Unfortunately, for several years in succession, as they made their way

in the procession from the Honeybournes to Evesham, they were attacked by men from Evesham. There was serious rioting with many severe injuries and some people were killed.

The people of both Honeybournes appealed to the Pope in 1442 who, with an eye to his coffers, said that they need not join the Evesham procession but they still had to give the money (a farthing) that they would have put in the collection plate.

PEBWORTH - Strange goings-on at Pebworth House

Pebworth House is a large property in the centre of the village of the same name. It dates back to the 1600s but over the years there have been Georgian and Victorian additions.

Debbie lived there for many years and says:

There were lot of stories about the place. It was always said there was an underground passage from Pebworth House to

Above top: Seyne House in the 1800s.
Above lower: Honeybourne Church.

the church because it was a sanatorium and they didn't want to take the bodies out into the street, so an underground passage was built.

That's the only place where I had a clear vision of the things in it. This lovely old man would come and sit by the fireplace and I would talk to him in my head. I could feel him most of the time and sometimes I could see him. He was wearing a granddad shirt and an old brown jacket full of ash from his pipe. He told me all sort of things. He said his name was Charlie and he had been a patient in the sanatorium for many years with a bad cough. He had come back looking for his mate. I would have liked to have had really long conversations with him but we were always disturbed by the door or the 'phone.

After we had a new bathroom put in I saw him sitting by the stairs, looking miserable. I asked him, 'What's the matter?'. He said, 'It's all wrong, what they have done' and he said that he had discovered a leak. Next thing, there really was a leak and we had to get the plumber back.

He would move things. I would put the polish on the table and the next second it would be somewhere else. He would change the pictures round, I would come down in the morning and the pictures would be in the wrong places.

We would hear him moving around in the attic and there would be a heavy smell of tobacco at the top of the house. At nights I could hear a rustling noise like that of a silk dress going past.

My husband saw a ghost too. He was in the bathroom when he was joined by a lady in what he described as, 'a long white nightgown'. He said she looked as if she was encased in glass. He freaked out and he came rushing out with a towel wrapped round him. He wouldn't go back to live in the house after that. It broke up our marriage.

ABBOTS SALFORD - Salford Hall

Salford Hall has the date 1602 over the porch but the hall was built before then, probably in the fifteenth century for the Abbots of Evesham. The hotel guide says that it could have been built when Richard Hawkesbury was abbot, 'like many a mediaeval Friar Tuck he was noted for good living'. From 1807 to 1829 it was occupied by a community of Benedictine nuns who had been forced to leave Cambrai because of the French Revolution. They converted the hall into a girl's boarding school.

Jenny Williams worked at the hall for eighteen years for the last owner.

He used to say that he was just the Custodian, and he did his best to keep it as it was.

Lots of peculiar things used to happen. A smell used to hang around

Salford Hall on a wintry after-noon.

some of the rooms for hours, then it would just go. It was a horrible smell but not chemical and not sewage. The custodian tried everything, he brought in Rentokil and the sewage people but there was never any explanation. Then we had an elderly gentleman who said, 'I know what that is, it's the stuff they used to treat saddles with'. The front part of the house used to be stables.

At that time my grandson was about five. He used to wander over and come and see me. If you look at the front of the house, you will see a room with a round window. He came out of that bedroom and said, 'Them girls won't play with me'. I went into the room to have a look but it was empty. I went down to reception and everyone had gone. Nobody was there. I asked him, 'When you saw the girls in there what did you say to them?' He had said, 'Do you want to play?'. I asked him, 'What did they say?'. He told me that they just nodded their heads.

I left it at that. You don't want to pressure them too much at that age. It might frighten them.

Jenny's husband, Paul, goes past the hall regularly

When I walk my dogs I go across the front of the hall. About two years ago I saw two priests all dressed up in their black robes, going through the front door. When I got back home, I said to my wife, 'Have you got a christening there or something?'. She asked why. I told her that two priests had just gone into the hotel. She went to have a look but couldn't see the two priests anywhere and no-one had seen them.

81

All this was forgotten, then about two months later, a woman said to my wife, 'Have you got a christening on?'. My wife said, 'No, why?'. She said two priests had just come through the front door. That backed up my experience.

SALFORD PRIORS – Jasmine Cottage

This lovely old house is much too large to be called a cottage. Now occupied by Jane and her family, they have researched the history of the house and discovered some interesting information. Jane says:

Years ago, there was a ford across the Avon, people used to come from Cleeve Prior with their various produce and especially with the salt. The name of the village was originally Salt-ford Priors. This house was the granary where the produce was stored, we have an exceptionally wide staircase. There used to be stables along the side of the house for Shire horses, with a tack room. I was in the land army and I used to shelter in the stables when it was raining. I used to think, 'I would love to live here one day'.

The house was made into residential accommodation many years ago We have a photograph of the cottage in the early 1900s when it was known as Jasmine Cottage. The name was changed before we arrived. Standing outside the front door of the cottage is Mrs Bachelor who was born in 1897.

We moved in about 37 years ago. Only two rooms were habitable, the kitchen and my bedroom. In the kitchen was the old black-leaded stove. When we renovated the house we tried hard to keep it looking like it did in the old pictures, for example, we used the same kind of window frames.

At that time I had my first baby who was only six months old. My husband used to go to the pub in the evening and whenever he went I could hear a baby crying. I would keep going up and down the stairs but my baby was asleep. I thought, 'It must be one of the neighbours' children, but I had to admit that we had no close neighbours. It was a plaintive cry, like that of a small child. It only ever happened when my husband was absent. I thought 'Am I going mad? I have got to tell someone'. Then my mum did some babysitting. When I came back from my evening out, she said, 'I thought I was going mad. I have been up and down those stairs all night thinking I heard a baby crying. I said, 'Thank God for that. I thought I was going mad'. It went on for several years then it stopped.

Our stairs go up vertically and the children's bedroom is straight ahead. There's an oak door at the bottom of the stairs that creaks when you open it. We were always careful to close it at night in case of fire or something. One night we were lying in bed when I heard the door open. I said to my husband, 'Did you hear that?'. He said that he did. Then there was thump, thump, thump, the sound of heavy footsteps coming up the stairs. I said, 'There's someone coming up the stairs'. My husband said, 'I know'. You could tell by the creak which stair he was on. I said, 'They're nearly at the top, they're going to get to my son'. With that I jumped out of bed. I thought they were going to get my precious baby. No-one was there but there was an ice cold feeling at the top of the stairs. It was absolutely terrifying.

Another evening, I was downstairs with my neighbour, we were having a coffee and the children were asleep upstairs. Then we heard thump, thump, thump. We were both scared to death. I went upstairs with a poker in my hand.

The first bedroom that we had was above the kitchen. It had been

Jasmine cottage with Mrs Bachelor in the doorway.

83

shut off from the rest of the house and was full of straw. When we cleared it out we found an old metal chest, and a brass bed. We kept the bed and we sleep in it now. Even to this day we regularly hear the bed creak and make a noise as if someone has sat on the bed and been kicked off.

On one occasion my husband was standing in the kitchen doorway, talking to me. In the kitchen is one of the old-fashioned dressers and the top shelf has a ledge all round it. I had put an old pate dish up there. Suddenly it flew over the ledge and hit the floor with such force that it smashed to pieces, taking the handle of a serving dish off on the way down. How did that happen?

I have heard the voice of a little boy playing in the front room, and my daughter has seen an apparition twice. The first time, she woke up in the middle of the night, propped herself up on her elbow then noticed a hazy figure at the bottom of the bed wearing a Victorian dress with a narrow waist. The apparition floated back through the wall and disappeared. Then only a couple of months ago, she had been ill and she was upstairs when she saw a mass of moving particles beginning to form a long apparition, starting from the top down. She rushed downstairs to fetch me, calling 'Come and have a look at this'. By the time I got upstairs it had gone but the room was icy cold.

My husband has also seen a Victorian lady. He heard the bedroom door open and saw a figure in the doorway. Although he could only see it halfway down he could make out that it was a female. He just rolled over and went to sleep.

A very elderly woman lived in the village in a caravan and she was always knitting woolly socks. I don't know what she did with them all. Anyhow, she walked into my kitchen and said, 'You have a presence in this house'. I thought she must have had one too many, then she said, 'I'm a medium. The lady's name is Mary, you don't need to worry about her, she's very friendly and she loves your flowers. She will always be here'.

My three young children were in bed one evening when my younger daughter began screaming her head off. I went up to her and said, 'Will you go to sleep?'. She was hysterical. She kept saying 'The lady's been, she's gone through that wall'. I went to have a look at my son, who was then four years old, and he was having a convulsion. He ended up in hospital. I have often wondered since, did Mary come to warn us?

I went into the churchyard at Salford Priors with my neighbour, and something made us search a forgotten corner. There was a tombstone to Mary and George of Abbots Salford and they were buried with seven of their children. It didn't give any more information. I often wondered if it was the Mary who lived here. At that time, there were not all that many people living in this village.

The flying sugar bowl

A neighbour of Jane's also has problems:
A couple of years ago several strange things happened in our house. A glass sugar bowl just flew off the table and smashed on the floor. It landed with such force! The sugar went everywhere. A couple of weeks later, I was washing up, I put the washing up liquid on the draining board and it flew off.

We have an old cottage with a downstairs bathroom at the bottom of the stairs. I came out of the bathroom, something caught my eye and there was a lady standing at the bottom of the stairs dressed in Victorian clothes. Her dress was black and her face was in darkness so she was almost like a silhouette. It unnerved me for a few seconds. I didn't tell anyone as my son was twelve years old and I didn't want to upset him.

I haven't seen anything before or since.

Morgan rides again

Jane's daughter, Nicola's, owned a horse, Morgan, a much-loved old cob.
He died a couple of years ago when he had reached the ripe old age of 34. I had him when I was only sixteen.

When he became very old we retired him, I gave him a pat and said, 'I'm not going to ride you any more' and we left him to enjoy himself in the field. But he wouldn't accept retirement. He used to stand at the gate – he pushed it so hard he bent it – and whine. Sometimes his whinnying was almost a scream.

We had had his body taken away and we bought some new horses. About a week after he died I went on a ride for about an hour with my mum and when we came back up the lane both mum and I heard Morgan whinnying as clear as day. We both stopped, tears streaming down our faces.

The peeping housewife

Another lovely anecdote from Salford Priors:
My husband had been down to the pub. When he came in, I woke up and, half asleep, I watched him getting undressed and was a bit

cross to see him just dropping his clothes on the floor. The next morning I said to him, 'I saw you last night, dropping your clothes on the floor'. He said, 'I didn't, I hung them up'. When I checked in our bedroom, there they were, all on hangers. So who was it that I saw getting undressed?

Abbots Salford and the God Pan

In medieval times and up until about 1850, people saw goblins, fairies, elves, pixies, demons, puck, and even the devil. Roy Palmer's *The Folklore of Worcestershire* has a long list of devil-based stories. These strange creatures are now rarely mentioned but here, at last, is one of them.

Joy was born in Abbots Salford and lived in a cottage at the far end of the village.

When I was six years old, I used to go to bed at 6.30. The light in my room was switched off but the landing light was left on so that I could see. My sister slept in the next room,

I was lying there, with my eyes wide open when I saw this thing sitting on the edge of the bed, a figure with curly horns, half man, half goat. I thought it was the devil. It was leaning over the bottom of the bed and was brown and fluffy and about the size of a man. It was looking at me with a mischievous expression, sort of leering. I was terrified. I kept staring at it, then it bent down and pinched my big toe, so I not only saw it, I felt it. I screamed and screamed. My dad came in and said I must have been dreaming.

I kept playing it over and over again in my mind. At one point I said to a Catholic friend of mine, 'Can I come with you to you church?. So I went to the Catholic church for a little while to try and get rid of the image of the devil.

A few years ago I went to see my uncle and we were talking about the old days.

I asked him. 'Did you ever see any ghosts?'. Then he said he had seen something that looked over the wall in the front of Salford Hall, with its elbows on the wall. He said, 'I was scared stiff. I was on my bike so I threw my bike into a ditch and ran hell for leather. When he described it, it was the same as the thing I saw. He said, 'Why didn't you say something?'. I said, 'Nobody would believe me'.

I have since been to Italy and over there they have

The God Pan   sculptures like the man I saw. It's Pan, the god of

86

shepherds and hunters, and flocks and herds, and the personification of nature.

I still think about it and sometimes I wonder if I was dreaming but on the other hand, I'm sure I wasn't.

In memoriam

One of the villagers, Chris, has a story about a local character:

About 30 years ago we had a man living in the village known as Des. He was a slow learner, an epileptic and he had a disabled hand. I have been told that he had his first epileptic fit when his mother died – he was only a schoolboy. I remember when she died, it was so sad. They took the coffin to the church on a cart and there were two little boys, Des and his brother, walking behind it. His dad married again and his step-mum looked after them.

Des was so good-hearted. He would come round to see if you wanted any errands doing. He didn't bother about the money – if you gave him a fag at the end of the week he was quite happy. He just wanted something to do. He would even walk the four miles (6km) to Bidford if you needed a prescription. I used to work at Stratford and I didn't like walking back from the bus stop in the dark so he used to meet me every night at 6.30 off the bus at Salford church. You could always hear him coming because he wore hob-nailed boots and he would run rather than walk.

My parents lived next door to me. My dad was a market gardener and he had a white van which he parked between our houses. Early one morning, I came out to go work while dad was loading up his van. I came between the two houses and heard Des's hob-nailed boots coming down the road. As he went past he called out, 'Hiya Fred'. I said to my dad, 'You're a bit stuck up, aren't you?', My dad asked, 'Why?'. 'Des has just spoken to you and you didn't answer him'. My dad asked, 'Did you see him?'. 'No', said I, 'I only heard him'. 'What are you talking about' said my dad, 'He's dead'.

I had heard that he'd died but I'd momentarily forgotten. He was quite young, mid-fifties if that. No doubt he's up there now, running errands for everyone in his hob-nailed boots.

Many thanks to Jane of Jasmine Cottage for inviting her friends, relatives and neighbours for a session of ghost story-telling.

9. KIDDERMINSTER

o other town has as many famous murders as Kidder-minster. Way back in the 1200s, the king was nearly mur-dered here. Henry III was staying with John Biset, Lord of the Manor of Wolverhampton in his Residential Hall in Kidderminster, in the Dudley Street/Orchard Street area. Also staying at the Hall was a relative of Biset's, Mar-garet. She was 'at her devotions' at midnight when she heard a noise and realised that an assassin was making his way to the king's chamber. She raised the alarm and the king was saved.

Shooting down the cavalry

The parliamentarians won the Battle of Worcester in 1651, consequently hundreds of royalist cavalry were fleeing from the battle. Many of them de-cided to escape through Kidderminster. About 30 of Cromwell's troops who had been guarding Bewdley bridge heard about it, rode to Kiddermin-ster and stood in the market place. As the galloping horses approached, they fired. In the dark and confusion the royalist cavalry had no idea that they were only facing an army of 30. There was a great confusion with bul-lets flying everywhere, many men and horses were injured and several were killed.

The Lady of the Night

There's an old story that, in the 1600s, where the present town hall now stands, was an inn of bad repute, the haunt of ladies of the night and gin-sodden mothers. When one of the customers left the pub he discovered that his wallet was missing and realised the prostitute had stolen it. He rushed back into the pub, the prostitute's husband woke from a drunken slumber, fired his gun and accidentally shot his wife, then realising what he had done, he shot himself. The story goes that a well-dressed man can be seen at midnight on dark nights outside the town hall, patting the ground as he looks for his wallet.

The murder of Francis Best

In an area near the canal just off New Road there was once a corn mill known as Caldwell Mill. The miller's name was Francis Best and every

Saturday morning at 9.30 am prompt Francis would walk from the mill, over Spring Grove (where the West Midlands Safari Park now stands) to Bewdley market. On 8th June 1771 he was set upon by John Child, a journeyman weaver, described as an idle ne'er-do-well, easily recognisable because of a club foot. When the body was recovered, it was found that the killer had overlooked 65 gold sovereigns in the waistcoat pocket! Sometime later Child returned to Kidderminster to buy a horse on which to escape, but he was recognised and apprehended. He was hung on 18th July and his body was sent for dissection. While awaiting trial, Child was held in heavy shackles in Spring Grove mansion, and it is said that from time to time the sound of a shackled and injured foot being dragged across the floor can be heard in the upper storeys of the house.

Two confessions but no arrest

Until recent times, Cobham Road was known as Aggborough Lane. This is where the body of a hop-picker, savagely mutilated, was discovered in October 1903. Jack the Ripper had been at work only fifteen years previously and panic raged. The strange fact is that although there were several arrests and two people confessed, no-one was charged. The first written confession was in January 1904 when George Fisher was taken to Lincoln prison, charged with vagrancy. A diary was found in his possession in which he had written: 'I murdered Mary Swinford on Saturday evening first in October at Kidderminster, Worcestershire. God help me. Murder will out some day'. However, at the trial he was able to prove that at the time of the murder, he was in South Molton in Devon.

Kidderminster Town Hall, A double murder is said to have taken place on this site.

A second confession came in 1914 from Alfred Kimberley in Canada. It was decided that he had confessed to get a free passage to England where he could clear his name.
(More details are in Foul Deeds and Suspicious Deaths Around Worcester.*)*

Killed on active duty

Kidderminster is well-known for its carpets. From medieval times the town had been famous for its cloth weaving, then, in 1735, John Pearsall and John Broom wove their first carpet. The population rose from about 3,000 in 1700 to about 8,000 in 1811 and an enormous 17,000 in 1851. The industry was plagued by disagreements between the carpet masters and the carpet weavers, and strikes were frequent. The carpet weavers were a militant crowd and their conduct at elections was beyond belief.

This was a time when only approximately seven people in every hundred were rich enough to vote, and as voting was not done in secret, everyone knew where the loyalties of the voters lay. There were two main parties, Liberal known as Whig, and Conservative known as Tory.

In 1855 and 1856 Robert Lowe (Whig) was elected unopposed as MP. He had risen to become vice chairman of the Board of Trade. Then in 1857, the local solicitor, William Boycott, had decided to stand against him. Boycott had helped the weavers during a recent strike and was very popular.

The editor of *Berrows Worcester Journal* should have taken some responsibility for the riots because of his inflammatory language. He described Lowe's election address as follows:

His laboured speech ... was nothing more than a fulsome panegyric on Lord Palmerston who had given him so comfortable a berth on the Board of Trade.

After remarking that the speech had upset the Wesleyans, the churchmen, the economists, the educationalists, the tax payers, death abolitionists, free traders and peace lovers, he concluded with: 'The electors should pause before they send to Parliament a man whose political conduct is guided entirely by consideration of self'.

Hustings. A satirical picture by Hogarth representing a scene on the hustings during polling

A wooden platform, the

90

'Hustings', was always built specially for the elections. From here, candidates were nominated, they made their election speeches, polling was declared open, and the results were announced. Unfortunately the mayor had decided that the Hustings should be built in an open area near to the church, and this was where the broken stones were held for road building. Two polling booths had also been erected.

The week before the election it was obvious that trouble was brewing. The streets were full of noise and shouting and the night before the elections were held, the windows of the Swan Hotel were broken and some police officers were attacked.

At two o'clock, on the last Saturday in March, the factories closed and 8,000 carpet weavers poured into the streets. At first they gathered round the polling booths. Voters only managed to get to the booths with police assistance. As soon as the state of the polls began to be revealed, anyone who voted for Lowe was grabbed, spat on, punched and kicked. Samuel Brome, a carpet master, was one such person. While he was on his way to see a friend a foundryman grabbed him and hit him while another began kicking him.

As time drew near for the polls to be closed and the results announced, the mob moved to the hustings. The crowd was getting ugly and stones began to be thrown. Some women were holding up the edges of heir pinafores to make a basket and filling them with stones. Boycott left and advised Lowe to do the same. Lowe's friends offered to take him to a place of safety but his supporters were anxious for a traditional ceremonial procession to go ahead.

When Boycott's defeat was announced, the crowd was furious. There were shouts of 'Come out and let us kill the ----'. Facing the crowd estimated at 8,000 were 13 police officers including the special constables. They formed a line in front of the hustings.

The mob continued to throw stones. One of the Conservatives was hit on the head and the blood poured. Robert Lowe himself was hit on the head and his grey hair was red with blood. Lowe and six of his supporters tried to get into the church but there were men on the steps throwing stones. They tried to get into a large house nearby but the gates were locked. They ran along the wall, found an unlocked door at the back of the house scrambled in and bolted themselves in. At half past four the police managed to get Mr Lowe and the mayor away.

Police Constable Jukes were carried into the house unconscious. He had been cut all over his body. His nasal bone was fractured and his skull lacerated.

At 5 o'clock the mayor telegraphed Birmingham for assistance. A troop of the tenth hussars arrived on horseback at ten minutes to midnight, formed up in the yard of the Lion Hotel and the mayor read the riot act. The hussars policed the streets until 4am.

The surgeon announced that Jukes was in an unsatisfactory condition. A local antiquarian, Ebenezer Guest, says that he died a few days later, however, we can find no record of his death. If anyone could throw any light on this mystery we would be grateful. The publisher's address is at the front of the book.

The ringleaders were fined, among them were John Hayes, John Cook, James Tranter and James Slater who were fined thirty shillings each. It was proposed that the reserve force of eight at Worcester should be increased.

Them boots just keep on walking

The Sutton Arms pub in Sutton Park Road is still there on the south western side of Kidderminster offering live music and good beer. When Peter Finch was a young lad, about ten or twelve, he used to play round the back.

In those days there was a grassy area set against the wall of the pub. It's a car park now. I lived just down the road and the others lived locally – we just used to lark about.

One hot sunny afternoon, I think it would have been the summer of about 1973, my mate Kevin and I were on a pathway and leaning against the wall, looking down on to the grassy area, when suddenly a pair of army boots, about size 10, just appeared halfway along the grassy area and marched across as if there was somebody in them. They walked straight into the wall and disappeared.

We were more amused than anything.

The ground behind the pub, Foley Park, was once an army training centre.

The haunted boots on their way across the back of the Sutton Arms pub.

The phantom of the loo

The next story by Julie in Kidderminster was heard on local radio in a programme hosted by Andrew Easton on 31st October 2008. The strange thing is that we have more ghost stories from lavatories than from graveyards. Julie was yet another victim of the phantom of the loo.

We live in a Council house. Every now and then, a person comes through the house and goes into the outside toilet. It's a gentleman in a black cloak, a long black jacket, and a black hat. He doesn't sit on the toilet, he just stands there. Sometimes you wake up in the night and go to the toilet and see that figure, it's there. It's a bit like a sixth sense, just a shadow.

I'm not scared because my husband is a mariner and we've five lads. We have all seen it several times. One of my boys came home and said, 'Hullo dad', he thought it was his dad, but his dad was sitting in the living room.

Her husband added:

The ghost in the loo. Figure taken from a Victorian painting.

93

The toilet was built in concrete after the war. It's been there for sixty-odd years. The house has the outside toilet, a coal bunker and a shed for bikes and garden equipment made out of breeze blocks with a flat concrete roof but they're all part of the house.

We haven't told anybody about it. It's a bit of a nuisance. Sometimes things go missing and when you don't need them any more they turn up. I was looking for a systems disc once to format the hard disc and couldn't find it anywhere. Eventually I got another copy, then it turned up.

We last saw the gentleman a couple of months ago.

The resurrected poodle

Those who have lost one of 'man's best friends', find some solace in this kind of story:

We have had a number of poodles in our life, the first one was in 1967. The last one we had, Kiri, died in 2006. She was very affectionate. As she got older she lost her strength. One of her favourite places was under the wing of the settee because she had to lean against the arm of the settee to stand up. In the end she was messing everywhere so we had to take her to the vet and have her put down. It was the kindest thing we could do.

Some months later my husband was working in the kitchen and I was sitting in the lounge when I happened to glance across the room. Kiri was standing there, under the wing of the settee; she was in good health and standing very upright. As soon as she saw that I had seen her, she just vanished. I called out to my husband, 'I've just seen Kiri'. It was very comforting.

The authority on Kidderminster ghosts and murders is Alan Lauder, who now runs the Balloon shop in Coventry Streeet as well as Kidderminster Ghost Walks. For the cost of a few balloons he will regale you with more details of most of the above ghost stories.

10. THE MALVERN HILLS

igh up in the 15th century stained glass windows of Malvern Priory is the picture of a murder taking place. Saint Werstan is seen sticking his head out of a window while a bearded and uniformed man, possibly a Celt, is standing by with raised sword, about to chop off his head. This is a pictorial record of the eleventh century martyrdom of Saint Werstan, thought to have occurred near St Anne's well. The story goes that the murder led to the foundation of the Abbey. Two men, Guido and Aldwyn, were somehow involved in the murder. Aldwyn planned to go on a pilgrimage to Jerusalem, perhaps to get absolution, but before he went he had to get permission from bishop Wulstan, later Saint Wulstan. The bishop asked him to stay and 'do gret things for Malvern'. Aldwyn lived in Malvern as a hermit but was joined by other monks and the priory was established. It was definitely in existence by 1127 when the monks received a charter from Henry I.

The present Malvern Priory was originally a church for the monks, from which the general public were banned. The monks had built a tiny, plain church in front of the Priory, 90 feet by 36 feet (27m x 11m) for the general public. By the 1500s it had fallen into decay. Malvern folk looked upon the beautiful Priory Church with great envy. Their chance came when Henry VIII dissolved the monasteries. Although there were no more than 100 families living in Malvern at that time, they managed to raise the huge sum of £20 in 1541 to buy the Priory church for their own use. The gatehouse was converted into a charming little museum in 1979 after being damaged by a speeding icecream van.

The story has been told many times of the way in which Malvern was at the centre of one of the biggest scandals the monastic church has ever known. The Prior, William of Malmsbury, was keeping 22 women in farms and houses round about. The Bishop of Worcester heard about this; he threw William out and placed his nephew as Prior instead.

The window showing the martyrdom of St Werstan.

Over the centuries there had been a dispute as to who owned the abbey, Westminster or Worcester, so the Bishop despatched his nephew and a group of monks to the Archbishop at Westminster to get his blessing. Instead of blessing them, the archbishop threw them into prison where they were held in chains. The wrangling between the bishop and archbishop went on for over a year, it even came to the ears of the king and the Pope. All that time the Bishop's nephew was held in chains. Finally, the Abbey was given to Westminster but the Bishop of Worcester was given the Manor of Knightwick for his pains.

Odours of sanctity

In October 2008 Clare from Malvern told the following story on local radio. Perhaps she lives on the site of one of the houses which once belonged to Malvern Priory:

Let me set the picture. I can't cook. You never have any nice smell coming out of my kitchen unless it comes from the microwave.

We live in Malvern in a brand new house. About eight months after we moved in - about Eastertime last year, people were coming into the kitchen saying, 'Oh, that smells like hot cross buns cooking'. I could smell it too. I say, 'Right, but I'm not cooking hot cross buns'. But the other thing was, we had a lovely smell of roast chicken coming out of the kitchen. Then we could smell pipe smoke.

In the morning when we're eating our breakfast we get the sight of something, a flick of a skirt or something in the dining room. You think, 'I'm sure I saw something, oh, never mind'.

We recently discovered that our house was built on the site of an old convent, and our house is situated where the kitchens would have been.

The rise and fall of Dr Gully

In the mid 1700s Dr John Wall, working with a chemist from Worcester, was able to prove that Malvern water was exceptionally pure. Incidentally, Dr Wall also founded the Worcester Porcelain Company. Malvern became a spa. The Pump Room and Baths were built between 1819 and 1823, together with several grand hotels. By 1841 the population had increased to 2,768.

Dr James Wilson and Dr James Gully, created a sensation by introducing a new hydropathic treatment. Their therapy aimed at stimulating the circulation and driving out toxins from the body. Patients were woken at 5am, undressed, wrapped in wet sheets then blankets. After an hour they were unwrapped and buckets of water were thrown at them. This was followed by a five-mile walk sustained by a bottle of water and water from the wells. Then back home to a breakfast of dry biscuits and more water. For entertainment during the day the patient could select from a range of baths. Dinner was always boiled mutton and fish, followed by a few hours in bed but this time in a dry one.

Although Wilson and Gully were bitterly opposed by many medical men, by the mid 1840s they had set up treatment centres in the Crown Hotel, (Now Lloyds Bank, Belle Vue Terrace), Priestnitz House (now Park View, overlooking Priory Park) and in what is now the Tudor Hotel. The Priessnitx Hotel alone cost £18,000, and was named after the Czech who invented hydrotherapy. There were other similar clinics in Malvern but Wilson and Gully were the two most famous (and wealthy) practitioners.

It brought the rich and famous to Malvern. Among their patients were Queen Victoria, Queen Adelaide, William Gladstone (prime minister), Charles Dickens (author), Florence Nightingale (famous nurse), Benjamin Disreali (prime minister), George Eliot (novelist), John Ruskin (art critic), and Alfred Lord Tennyson (poet). Practitioners made a fortune, especially Dr Wilson and Dr Gully.

Dr James Manby Gully led an eventful life. He was born in 1808 in Jamaica, educated in Paris and, in 1829, attended the prestigious Edinburgh University as a medical student. This was a memorable year in the university's medical department. The lecturer, Robert Knox had been buying corpses at £10 a time to study anatomy and two Irish villains, William Burke and William Hare, had begun digging in the local cemeteries to provide the bodies. Worse still, they decided that it was easier to provide corpses by murdering the locals. Knox became suspicious when some of his cadavers were still warm. Burke was caught after his 15th victim and hung in 1829.

It so happened that at the University at the same time was Charles Darwin who shocked the world with his theory of evolution. Darwin had suffered from nervous dyspepsia for nearly ten years when, in 1949, after four months of vomiting, he turned to Dr Gully in desperation. He rented The Lodge in Worcester Road, Malvern and started a two-month trial. His health improved and he continued the treatment at home. Darwin's daughter, Annie, was ten years old and appeared to be suffering from indigestion. He took her to see Dr Gully on 24 March 1851. For the first week he stayed with her, then he left her in the doctor's care. Gully sent for Darwin urgently as Annie had developed a 'bilious fever' and although Gully assured Darwin and his wife that Annie was improving, she died on 23 April. Her death certificate reads 'Bilious fever with typhoid character'. She was buried in Malvern Priory. As for Darwin, he continued his treatment for some months, then stopped but began again several years later.

Twenty years later Dr Gully became involved in a scandal of international proportions. In 1872, he fell madly in love with one of his patients, twenty-two year old Florence Ricardo, and they became secret lovers. Dr Gully was 64 years of age and still married. Florence was a widow, her husband having died in mysterious circumstances, leaving her £40,000. The following year Dr Gully and Florence travelled together to Germany and Florence became pregnant. Dr Gully performed an abortion.

Two years later Florence married Charles Bravo. A mutual friend wrote to Gully, telling him of the marriage. He is reputed to have torn the letter to shreds in a rage. Florence and Charles Bravo were living at The Priory in Balham, London and Gully went to visit them. The marriage was not a happy one. Bravo was described as controlling, miserly and violent. He tried to get his hands on Florence's money, he repeatedly threatened the housekeeper with dismissal, and he sacked the groom. Four months into their marriage, in April 1876, Bravo was poisoned, and after three days in agony, he died. Leading doctors agreed that he had been given antimony, a toxic mineral from China. All the household were suspect, Florence, the housekeeper, the groom and, for a short time, Dr Gully. The culprit was never found and Dr Gully was finally cleared of any involvement.

Two years later Florence was dead from alcohol poisoning.

The verger's tale

This narrative goes back to 1996. We heard it quite by accident, when we went into a beautiful old church in Malvern to take photographs, and started chatting to the verger. He told us:

I have always thought that my aunt was an angel. My brother and I were abandoned when we were small and my aunt and uncle took us in and brought us up. We lived in a comfortable, pre-war house in Malvern. When we were in our late teens my aunt died but my uncle, brother and I worked well together, we were a team. After another eight or nine years my uncle died.

It was after my uncle's death that my aunt began putting in an appearance. I am a Christian, and I believe that we have spirits around us all the time, some good, some bad, so I am not unduly alarmed when I see her. In fact, I feel a very peaceful sensation. I believe that my aunt visits us because she is worried about us. I suppose it is very nice of her to worry about us and come back. What I should do is to talk to her, to reassure her and tell her that she is not to worry; we are alright, but I must admit I am too apprehensive to do that. I don't want her to know that I can see her and I just ignore her.

I see her sitting on my bed most nights when I go to bed but I just turn over and go to sleep. I know that she is there watching me during the day because I feel this cold sensation just a little way from my face. People tell me it must be a draught but how can you have a draught when the door is shut and the windows are closed? My brother sees her more often than I do, he is very sensitive to this sort of thing. He, too, ignores her, we say that she has had her life, now we are going to get on with ours. Two or three times she has been joined by my uncle and once they even brought the dog! There was my aunt, uncle and the dog all crowded into my little bedroom. We have had the house blessed twice, not so much for our sake but for hers, to send her on to her final resting place. Each time, she has gone for a few months but then she's back

I believe that we live with these spirits all around us, sometimes we see them, sometimes we don't, some spirits are good, others are bad and throughout life we gradually move towards the spirit world until we become part of it at death.

The ghost of Warwick House

Warwick House was a high-class Victorian departmental store in the centre of Great Malvern. It closed down in 1992 and has been converted into apartments. The story of its ghosts was told by the maintenance engineer, Frank, and has created so much interest we make no apologies for repeating it here:

I started there in about 1977. They had a ghost there – it was a lady. She seemed to be particularly interested in newcomers. Sometimes, a new girl would be down in the lower area where the kitchens and the tea bar were and this Victorian lady would appear and disappear. They usually grabbed their coats and never came back. It was difficult to get a description of her because a lot of the girls who saw her left straight away. From what I understand, she was wearing dark clothing and they usually described it as Edwardian, which I assume meant a long skirt and puffed sleeves. She was of a late middle-age. Occasionally, the every-day staff would see her too. One girl was particularly prone to this sort of thing and saw her several times.

I used to be working all hours and would often be in the store at nine o'clock at night when everybody had gone home. I never saw her although I felt her presence. There was one particular area at the top of the building where I used to feel that someone was watching me and I would turn round and be surprised to find that nobody was there. In the end I ignored the feeling, it didn't bother me. A lot of people felt a presence there. I had a workshop down in the basement and I used to make certain that I closed all the cupboards before I left at night because of the tools and other equipment, but when I went back in the morning the cupboards would be open. This only happened for the first few months I was there.

We had an Alterations Room. I was working in there one day and taking down some very old fittings when there was a smell of lavender perfume. It was very strong, almost as if someone was standing there, watching. It was an old-fashioned perfume, very heavy. The girls had smelt it before, it used to come and go.

At the end of the ladies' underwear department were several fitting rooms where the lingerie was hanging on metal hangers on a chrome base. As you moved the hangers along they made a scraping noise. Several of the girls heard this noise and went into the fitting rooms to investigate. The hangers had been moved along but no-one was there.

We got to like her in a way. Apart from one or two loud crashes she was never any trouble. We asked around to see if anyone had any idea who she was. Nobody could remember anything terrible happening there like an accident or a murder. The only thing they could think of was that back in Victorian times some of the staff used to live in, there were six or seven little rooms for them up in the Gods. We thought it might be one of the old staff who was reluctant to leave.

Just before the place closed down one or two strange things happened. In the same department where I had felt her presence (ladies' underwear and night-dresses) were two large fitting rooms. At nine o'clock one night there was an almighty crash. I rushed upstairs, thinking that the ceiling had fallen down or something, but not a thing was out of place.

Since the store closed there have been no more reports of the ghost. She was certainly very sociable and perhaps she decided to leave when the place was empty.

Are you being served?

There's a sequel to this story. After the author had been telling ghostly tales at a Malvern meeting a few years ago, Monica Alison came forward and said that she had been one of the staff living in a tiny room above the main entrance. She had heard rumours about the ghost but never encountered it.

This is her account of life at Warwick House. At weekends, she was allowed to return to her home in Castle Morton.

Warwick House in Great Malvern has now been converted into

Warwick House just before it was converted into apartments.

flats, but it used to be a departmental store and I was a trainee, living in, for seven years. There were two fashion shops in Malvern, Warwick House and Kendall's which stood where the Halifax is now. The trainees at Kendall's were known as Kendall's Girls whereas those at Warwick House were known as Warwick House Young Ladies. We were definitely more up-market!

I started working there as a dressmaker in 1944, I was the first trainee towards the end of the war. During the war the store had not been allowed to make clothes. Over the next twelve months I was joined by more trainees until in the end there were about a dozen of us. There were all kinds of work-rooms. There was one room making school uniforms and clothing for schools, then there was the workshop for men's wear and the lingerie shop. I was in model gowns which was chiefly bridal wear and ball gowns.

The store was owned by Mrs Mitchell. She was quite Victorian, she was only small but she was very intimidating. You wouldn't think of passing either her or a senior staff member on the stairs. You would wait at the bottom until she had come down, then you would go up. If you passed her on the stairs you would have been reprimanded.

I started work there when I was fourteen and we had to be in bed with lights out by nine o'clock. As you grew older so you were allowed a later bed-time but not until you were twenty-one were you allowed to stay up until eleven o'clock. We were allowed two late passes each week. For those we had to get written permission from our parents and get it signed by our boss and by Mrs Mitchell. I think it had to be signed by the Welfare Supervisor as well. We had to go past the Welfare Supervisor's room each morning and show her our hands and our shoes to make sure they were clean.

Warwick House catered for all of the arrangements for a wedding. These were really grand weddings, with up to six bridesmaids. Warwick House even sold furniture for the house of the bride. Mrs Mitchell owned the Mount Pleasant Hotel opposite and various members of the bridal party would sometimes come and stay at the hotel for a week while they were being measured up.

I played truant once. I hadn't been very well and was confined to my room but the local cinema was showing the life of Chopin - 'A Song to Remember' and I had wanted to see it for some time. My friend said, 'Come on, let's go'. She took my coat for me while I crept down the flight of steps between Warwick House and the Tudor Hotel next door and went off to the cinema. It was a nightmare. Every time the lights went up I sank down in my seat, terrified in case someone from Warwick House was there who would recognise me. I said to my friend, 'We'll have to creep out before the end because, when the lights go up, we'll have to stand up to sing 'God Save the King' and I will be seen'. If anyone had noticed me there, I would have got the sack.

My boss was an absolute perfectionist. You couldn't have a hair or a crease out of place. And, if she showed you something for the first time on one day, you were expected to do it to perfection the next day. She showed me how to do arrowheads at the top of a pleat. I thought, 'I'll practice that tonight'. In those days we had gas lights, I put my light out, but later, I put it on again and sat up in bed practising this arrowhead. Our housekeeper was Austrian, Mrs Ricetti, she was a dear. I heard someone creeping about outside, then the door opened and there was Mrs Ricetti. She said, 'Monica, you naughty girl, what are you doing?'. I said, 'I've got to practice this needlework for tomorrow'. She said, 'Be a good girl and put the light out and go to sleep'. I think I put the light on again later. I had to have the arrowhead just right.

Although my boss was a perfectionist, she did used to leave things until the last minute. Sometimes a bride would be waiting anxiously for her dress to be finished. One of the brides was staying at the Foley Hotel and the wedding party was starting out from there, so I had the job of delivering the dress. I was only tiny when I was fourteen and the dress was in a huge cardboard box. I staggered up to the hotel where there were revolving doors. I wasn't used to revolving doors and I went sprawling across the carpet. I felt such a fool.

The store had a reputation of being haunted. I must say that I had an uneasy feeling when I went down to the basement. The fur stores and carpet stores were there - I didn't sleep very well and sometimes I could hear the door being drawn across, it was a sliding door. It was very spooky. No-one else heard it.

I really enjoyed my time there. We were invited to big balls at various hotels and there were big bands at the Winter Gardens. Although it was only just at the end of the war we were all in evening dress. As I was a dressmaker I could make my own. It was all very grand. To me it was the good old days when we lived in the grand manner. Everything had a value then, these days they don't value anything.

Wanna see my headlights?

Stonemason Oliver Webb has a great repertoire of ghost stories. Here is one of them.

The only "odd" incident that came to mind recently was to do with a pair of car headlights that I bought a few years back. We're brewing up for a loft conversion and I've been forced to rationalise my mountains of treasures up there before either they come crashing through the ceiling, or the builders turn up on the doorstep! Anyway, I digress, the headlights are a pair of brand new Peugeot 204 items which I bought about 15 years ago for my pet car. The lamps were brand new "old stock" of some 20 years' vintage and were still packaged in their original and quite stout cardboard cartons. Both lights were perfect when I picked them up, and still perfect when I got them home. Their perfection continued unabated for several days whilst they were stored lovingly in a cupboard safe from harm's way (204 headlights, you must understand, are terribly hard to come by, and a pair of new ones represented a major coup!). About a week after they were lovingly stashed away, I gently lifted them out to show a like minded friend (we car bods are easily amused - "Wanna see my headlights....?"). The headlight in the top box was just as perfect as the day it had been lovingly tucked up, but the one beneath was smashed to bits - not cracked, or just broken, but literally smashed to a thousand pieces. Yet the box had remained unopened and untouched since I'd put it there, and there wasn't a mark on the box. Whatever/whoever it was that broke my precious light was not popular! I was living alone in a top floor flat to which nobody else had access.

The only other annoying thing that happened there was a pair of watercolour paintings disappeared without trace. They were stored in a large specially constructed, deliberately anonymous-looking sleeve and kept in a drawer. I stil don't have the paintings and I'm still looking for a replacement headlight lens!!

11. THE PERSHORE AREA

ershore is in the heart of the fertile Evesham plain and produces much of the country's fruit and vegetables, but is particularly famous for it plums. The Pershore Yellow Egg was found growing wild in Tiddesley Wood in the early 1800s and by the end of the century, over 900 tons (tonnes) of the fruit was sold each summer. Other varieties include the Pershore Purple and the Pershore Emblem. The town now holds a month long plum festival throughout August.

Pershore Abbey and the naughty parishioners

A retired lady from Pershore booked for a weekend's mediaeval history course at The Hill Residential College in Abergavenny. A Saturday trip was advertised, but when she booked the tutors had not decided where they were going to take the party. Imagine her exasperation when she arrived at the Hill for the course and learned that the chosen destination was Pershore Abbey. Her husband was very surprised when she called in for a cup of tea on Saturday afternoon.

This shows the importance of Pershore Abbey historically. It could have been founded as long ago as 690, and was occupied by Benedictine monks by 792 when they received a charter from King Edgar. In its early days it was a wealthy monastery but lost many of its estates to Westminster. Even part of the town was granted to Westminster and the story goes that, annoyed by this, the monks built the parish church of St Andrew across the road so that they would have their own church and would not have to share the cathedral church with those citizens who now came under Westminster's control.

Pershore Abbey was a magnificent building, the same length as Tewkesbury Abbey. The nave reached the entrance gate. Henry VIII dissolved this wonderful edifice in 1539. All that we have left is a bit of nave (Norman), the crossing (Norman) over which soars the tower, the transepts (Norman), the chancel (between 1200 and 1239) and a modern apse. The piers and arches could be about 1,000 years old!

In the late 1400s the parishioners stole the great seal of the abbey, which was equal in importance to today's credit card. They forged various documents so that the bishop lost some of his rights. The culprits were hauled up before the courts in 1522. Their fate is unknown but they were probably hung.

105

The gamble - Haselwoods v Hudsons

On the west wall of the church are two tombs to the Haselwood family. Thomas Haselwood reclines on his tomb, with two large kneeling figures left and right. The effigies of Fulk and Dorothea Haselwood are missing on the second tomb of 1569 but against the tomb chest are paintings of ten children, six girls, three boys and one infant. The Haselwoods were great landowners between 1520 and 1745, and although they originally came from Yorkshire and Northamptonshire, they settled in Wick.

What a family they were! In 1622 when King James was on the throne, Thomas Haselwood was brought before the courts as a rebel. His son, Francis, was fined in 1630 for not accepting a knighthood offered by Charles I. However, during the civil war of 1642-1651, he seems to have backed the losing side and become a royalist. He was accused of sending provisions to the royalist garrison at Worcester and his estates were confiscated.

After eleven years of commonwealth rule, in 1660, Charles II came to the throne and Francis received his reward for supporting the royalists. He was

The Haselwood tombs. Upper photograph: late 16th century tomb of Thomas Haselwood (prone), lower photograph: tomb of 1569 showing three sons and six daughters.

made Sheriff of Worcester in 1633. His son, Thomas, was knighted in 1681 and appointed Sheriff of Worcester the following year.

In the 1770s they began selling up their various estates. The question is, why?

The late Charles Hudson, who lived in the Wick Manor, was told by his family that about 250 years ago there was a mega game of cards which ended up with the Haselwoods heavily in debt to the Hudsons. The Hudsons therefore came into ownership of the Manor House. In 1994, a couple of members of the Haselwood family called at Wick Manor and asked if they could look round the house as, in previous centuries, it had belonged to them. The same story had circulated in their family. Mr Hudson said that he would show them round the house but he wasn't going to play another game of cards!

It's always a shame to spoil a good story but unfortunately, the estates did not pass directly to the Hudsons from the Haselwoods. The Reverend Bernard Wilson held the Haselwood estates before they were acquired by the Hudsons. Was there a mega game of cards between the Haselwoods and the Reverend? Perhaps someone can come up with an explanation.

Incidentally, there were several manors of Wick, the present manor house is not the original one and only goes back to the 1500s, except for the stables. These are thought to be the remains of St Cuthbert's church going back to the early 1200s. The half-timbered frontage of Wick Manor was built in the 1920s as a memorial to the heir, Lieutenant Alban John Benedict Hudson MC. During the First World War, he fell in love and his parents thought he was too young to marry, so they asked his commanding officer to post him away from home. He was killed at the battle of Messines in 7 June 1917. His distraught parents also built houses for disabled ex-servicemen in the village.

ECKINGTON - Who is she?

Eckington is a tiny country village about three miles (4.5km) southwest of Pershore. Sometime between 410AD and 1066, the Saxons lived here, as the village is thought to be named after the local chief, Ecci. The 'ing' refers to his court, and 'tun' is a fence of pointed stakes surrounding the village. There is still a Saxon cross in the churchyard.

The village was well-known by travellers for, half a mile away was a ford and a ferry boat across the river Avon, used especially by monks travelling between the abbeys at Pershore and Tewkesbury. In 1440 the ferry boat was replaced by Eckington Bridge, which was in turn replaced by the present stone bridge in 1729.

A drawing of Eckington bridge in the 1800s.

The two hard-working ladies who run the Pershore Historical Society and Heritage Centre, with its many publications, were sorting through some old papers when they came across the following ghost story written by Mrs Peggy Pittkin. She was a local naturalist, writing and illustrating a book on wildlife in the Nafford area for which she was given an award. Unfortunately, she died in November 1993 or 1994 just before her book was printed. She lived at Nafford Lodge, Eckington. The two historians note that there was no date to show exactly when the story was written down.

Mrs Pittkin writes:

I first saw the ghost when I was saying goodbye to my nephew and niece as they were about to leave to return to South Africa, and I was round the back of the house, next to their car. My grand-daughter, Joanna, came through the back door at the top of a flight of steps, and behind her was another girl about the same age, somewhere between ten to thirteen years old. I couldn't tell her exact height as she was on the step above Joanne. They both stopped. I assumed that she was a friend of Joanna's who was going with her to her brother Paul's school sports near Hereford. She was dressed in a fawn coat with a dark velvet collar. The flared coat was worn over an off-white dress with a round neck and no collar. I remember thinking the dress looked grubby. Her hair was fair flowing to the shoulders, caught back with a band off her face and the hair was slightly wavy. Her eyebrows were darker than her hair, her eyes dark, her complexion pale, altogether a pretty face. I thought no more about it, intending later to ask my daughter who she was.

The relations left, I returned to my side of the house and my daughter came in to me a few minutes later asking if Joanna was with me. Here I did a curious thing. I was going to answer 'they are upstairs in the bedroom' when I checked my words, altering them to she is upstairs'. This was instantaneous with no further thought. Then Joanna came into the room. She was alone and at that point I realized that I had seen a ghost.

All I had seen was a very ordinary girl in everyday circumstances and utterly of this world. The clothes I should date between 1890 and 1910 when there was little change in style. There is no doubt in my mind that I saw her and at 8.30 am, which was hardly the witching hour. The circumstances were so normal, for I was involved mentally and physically with saying goodbye to my relations.

Other people have seen her. One day, on returning from shopping in Pershore as was my custom, I went into the sitting room to tell my husband, an invalid, the local gossip. Having prepared lunch I returned to the room and my husband said 'What a pretty dress Joanna was wearing'. Replying to him I said Joanna was not with me but at school. With this he became angry, thinking I was teasing him for some unknown reason. Suddenly while talking to him I realised that he had seen the girl, and said no more. The subject was never mentioned again between us. What is so curious is that the girl has always been in a different dress when seen by different people who always remember it in detail.

Previous to this sighting, in the early '70's my daughter, when in the garden, heard children's footsteps in the house as did the dogs. They all ran into the house and upstairs expecting to find her two children out of bed when they should have been asleep. They were, however, both in bed and fast asleep, not feigning it. My daughter just accepted that it was the girl. This is what is so extraordinary – it's all very normal. The girl is part of the house, almost accepted as a member of the family.

About two years ago my daughter had a friend staying in the house. The friend was looking out of her window when above the hedge alongside the drive she saw the head of a girl bobbing up and down as she skipped along the drive. For a moment she thought it was Joanneathen realized she was away at school. We explained the situation and she, too, calmly accepted the girl as our phantom.

The last person to date to see anything was Mrs Arnold who works for my daughter. She was cleaning in an upstairs bedroom at 3.30 pm, when she heard footsteps on the landing and a girl's voice. On going to speak to her she found no-one there. Later in the afternoon she asked me if we had a ghost. I don't like the word 'ghost', I prefer, 'spirit'. I then told her what I knew. She, too, accepted it as a normal happening.

What is it that appears? Who is she? Why does she appear at different times of the day, only to a few people. Why does the viewer accept her as part of everyday life? I have given this great thought over a period of many years. I have a feeling that there is a happy spirit around the house. Many people who have stayed here have remarked that the house has a happy atmosphere.

My theory is that she was a child who had a very happy childhood followed by an unhappy or tragic adulthood, so that her spirit in some way returned to the place where she spent the halcyon days of childhood and youth. Our knowledge of things that are not of this earthly world is so small. Perhaps there is a way in which some people when they die, can communicate with those they love. Others whose 'spirit', for want of a better word, revisit the place where they spent part of their life and are seen years later by a person who has had no connection to them or their family, did not even know of their existence, yet sees them going about their normal life.

I have researched the history of the house, mill and extinct village having been given many early photographs relating to the property. In one photograph taken in 1894 I recognised a young woman of about 20 years of age who was the image of the girl I saw.

12. Old Redditch Town

edditch probably began when workers, such as masons and ironworkers, arrived to help the monks and lay-brothers to build Bordesley Abbey. The Abbey probably began in 1136 or 1138, a time of civil war when the country was in such chaos that there are two foundation charters. It was founded either by a French count, Hugh de Waleran, (a bloodthirsty warrior), or the haughty Empress Maud, who ruled as queen for several years and terrified her courtiers by bellowing at them in a deep masculine voice. The ground given for the abbey was water-logged and boggy but the monks were experts in irrigation and set about draining it.

The name of the town first appeared in the 1200s when a Latin document called it 'de Rubeo Fossata' (from the red ditch). The Normans were undecided whether the abbey should be male or female and in 1247 called it both la Rededich and le Rededych. At times, the water in the ditches are a distinctive reddish-brown.

The black dog of Arden

Despite its unpromising origins, the abbey prospered on the wool trade and became the fifth richest monastery in England. In the early 1300s, the noble Guy of Warwick was forced to seek sanctuary in Bordesley Abbey from the king's wrath, the reason being that he had (he maintained accidentally) chopped off the head of Piers Gaveston, the king's favourite. Piers had nicknamed Guy 'The Black Dog of Arden' to which Guy had replied that one day Piers would feel the teeth of the black hound. Guy was finally poisoned by a friend of Piers in revenge and he was buried in the abbey in 1313.

Five-and-a-half centuries later, a young intellectual, James Woodward, arrived in Redditch as tutor to the prosperous Bartleet family, and he realised that the bumps and hollows of the Bordesley meadows suggested that a great monastery once existed there. He decided on a little amateur excavation and discovered several tiles which are now in St Stephen's church, and a stone coffin which he assumed belonged to the Black Dog of Arden. Evidently, valuable public artefacts disappeared in the 1860s in the same way that they do today, so James arranged for his friends to take three-hour watches throughout the night. He himself took the witching hour of midnight. As St Stephen's clock chimed twelve, he saw a large black dog on a nearby rise. He grabbed a crowbar and advanced, but the dog had disap-

...the embodiment of the spirit of the Black Dog of Arden'. Drawing by James Woodward. Also seen on the corner of each page.

peared. In the morning, one of his friends remarked that he had seen a large black dog during the night which mysteriously disappeared. Woodward describes it as 'the embodiment of the spirit of the swarthy Earl of Warwick'. More details are in the visitor's centre in the Bordesley Abbey meadows.

The black dog is not the only ghost seen on the meadows. Hooded monks abound together with phantom footsteps and female voices at the adjacent Forge Mill, There's even a Victorian tale of a night watchman seeing a great chasm opening up out of which poured fiery horses and a coach. You can't help wondering if he had dropped off to sleep.

Forge Mill - The young man and the monk

The late Walter Stranz said that the Bordesley Abbey meadows were acquired for the town for the town by trickery. Sometime in the 1950s he was a young and raw Vice Chairman of the Redditch Council's Finance Committee. The Chief Finance Officer was on holiday when Walter was summoned to the council offices on urgent business. The town clerk told him that the Bordesley Abbey meadows were up for sale (which was true) for a more £5,000, a bargain which had to be snapped up immediately. They could then be relicensed for building land so that a huge profit could be made. Walter signed the cheque. He later discovered that there was no hurry, sales of other parts of the meadows did not go through for several months. Furthermore, the meadows were immediately labelled Public Open Spaces so they could never be used for building.

The Council were surprised to discover that, with this £5,000 they had bought an old mill on the edge of the Bordesley Meadows. In later years it was recognised as a real prize as the only water-powered needle scouring mill still in existence. It's probably at least 400 years old and was originally an iron refining mill, later adapted for needle-scouring. The last packet of needles was scoured in 1958. A team of volunteers preserved and repaired the mill, now a tourist attraction.

The upper floor of the mill was used for fly dressing ie tying the coloured feathers onto the fish hooks, a task which required nimble fingers so the floor was chiefly occupied by young ladies. The story goes that one of the fly dressers had an affair with a manager and when he finally rejected her, she drowned herself in the mill pound. From there, her body was swept into the water wheel and cut to pieces. She now returns to the mill to find her missing body parts. The staff are certain that the mill is haunted. Doors open and close of their own accord and they can hear light footsteps tapping across the upper floor when the mill is closed to visitors. One night, the officil key holder, Jo-Ann, was called out to the mill by the police as the alarms had been activated. As she and her husband entered the building they heard two female voices on the upper floor but the place was empty.

The following anecdote was told at Webheath First School during a car boot sale on Saturday, 27 June 2009.

I used to live in Sillins Avenue and I had a friend, Billy Ledbury, who also lived in Batchley. This must have been in about 1976. Billy was courting a girl in Abbeydale and when I had been out for the evening I sometimes used to bump into him and we would walk home together. From Abbeydale there were two ways to get to Batchley. You could walk through the Abbey Hostel, where the old prefabs were (Sainsbury's is now on the site) or you could go past Forge Mill and along Windsor Road. This last route was the quicker.

Late one evening I bumped into him by the swimming baths. I took one look at him and I thought 'What on earth is wrong with him?'. He looked terrified. He said, 'You will never believe what I have just seen'. He told me that he had walked back from Abbeydale through the needle museum – over the bridge where the old mill pool was - and was just going along the side of the museum when a monk came out of Forge Mill and walked straight across the path in front of him and disappeared. He was walking in the direction of the old cemetary. The monk had a hood over his face and never spoke or looked at him.

It was a foggy evening, and I said to him, 'Are you sure it wasn't some mist or fog?' but he was certain. I asked him if he would be alright going home. He said, 'I will calm down now' and with that he went his way and I went mine.

Forge Mill, haunted by a spurned fly dresser

Billy Ledbury now runs a hotel in Blackpool. We have tried to track him down but failed. If he could get in touch with the publishers we would love to hear the story in his own words.

The disappearing toothpicks

Here are two stories from houses situated near to the meadows:

My father is in his eighties and has got Parkinson's now so you can't have a conversation with him. It was my grandmother who told me this story, my father never mentioned it to me.

The teenagers used to congregate in the meadows and their favourite spot was under the chestnut trees. They used to mess about there, as teenagers do. They were fooling about when they happened to see a figure. At first they thought it was somebody with a hood over their face but as it got nearer they saw that it was a monk. Now my dad was dead sceptic but he was really, really scared. He and his friends took to their heels and ran.

All sorts of funny things have happened in our house. On two occasions my husband has seen a lady pushing her bike through the bedroom wall. The first time he looked and he couldn't believe what he was seeing. When it happened a second time, it faded more quickly.

He said she was wearing long clothes. The land has now been levelled, so if she was pushing a bike up the hill that would be on a level
with our windows.

On another instance I had some gammon for my tea. The gammon
was stuck in my teeth and I didn't want to floss in case I disturbed a
filling. I thought , 'What I need is a toothpick – a cocktail stick will
do'. So I get a chair and looked on the top shelf for the box of cocktail
sticks but I couldn't find them anywhere. My mother had been to stay
and I had spent the morning tidying her bedroom, I had dusted and
remade the bed, tidied round and everything was back to normal. I
happened to go into her room and there, on one of the units was a box
of toothpicks. My mum has no need for them as she has false teeth and
in any case, I had been in the bedroom previously and tidied up and
they weren't there then. They were Canadian – now I have been to
Canada but I certainly didn't buy any toothpicks. I took them to work
and told the others about them and we passed them round. The girls
said, 'But this is an old box'. I put them in front of a cupboard and they
have now disappeared again.

The flying toothbrush

The next story was heard at Studley Car Boot in October 2008:
My house is not far from Bordesley Abbey and it's on a short rise.

I worked for a little while with Professor Ranz who did the excava-
tions for Bordesley Abbey and she said she would love to excavate
my ground but she didn't have the money. She told me that she had
found lots of old burned wood in the local woods, it looked as if it had
been the subject of a Viking raid.

I used to have a figure coming into my bedroom when I was in bed
at the weekend. At first, I thought it was my dad but then one weekend I saw it clearly. It was a figure wearing a long black cloak and his
face was blurred. My sister only saw him once, he was touching the
jewellery on my mother's dressing table. She screamed for my mum
to come. My mum didn't have any valuable jewellery. I didn't know
until ten years later that my other sisters had seen him too.

In our next house we felt we there was definitely something there.
The doorknobs used to rattle. You could see them twisting and shak-
ing. Sometimes we used to think it was the dog. I would say to my
husband, 'Let the dog in' and he would say, 'He's here, right by you'.

It never bothered us. One of my two daughters was going through
puberty and we thought it was probably something to do with that.

She came flying down the stairs early one morning and said that when she was in the bathroom, the bathroom cabinet was open and a tooth-brush came flying out. We said to her, 'If you are frightened, take the dog up with you'. Do you know, she took the dog up but he would not go along the landing.

We hadn't moved into the house long when I had to go into hos-pital. My husband was woken up in the night by a sweeping noise coming from the stairs. It sounded as if someone was brushing down the stairs. He thought it might by the old lady next door doing some cleaning and the noise was coming through the adjoining wall. The next morning, he said to her, 'Was that you sweeping your stairs in the middle of the night?' and she said, 'Oh no, I never get up in the night, I can't see in the dark'.

My husband finished his supper one night and brought the empty tray into the kitchen. It floated up into the air, turned over and settled on the floor. Another time, I had a bottle opener attached to the wall by a piece of string and I had put an inverted cup over it. The cup floated up, along, and slowly and carefully settled itself on the floor.

I had two daughters and they each had a horse. Sadly, the one horse had to be put down. It was killed in the field and buried there. My daughter said that after the horse had been buried, they were stand-ing there and at the other end of the field was the other daughter's horse. Suddenly, they noticed that there was another animal standing by the horse. As they went over to have a look, it disappeared.

My two daughters spent a lot of time looking for four-leaf clovers. When they had finished exercising and cleaning out the horses they would sit in the field, searching for them but they never found any. Then my older daughter died, and afterwards I saw four-leaf clovers everywhere. I don't go looking for them, they just appear at my feet in the grass. Now all my books have four-leaf clovers pressed in them.

Tales from the needle trade

Visitors to the town are amused to discover that, although the town is fa-mous for needle-making, no-one knows exactly when the needles arrived. The earliest record of needlemaking goes back to the 1630s and from then on, the town grew rapidly. Everyone wanted to get into the needle industry. A farm labourer earned about 70p a week whereas a needlemaker could earn as much as £3. In 1800 the population was about 1,000. In 1841, it was 3,314. In 1871 it was 6,737. Redditch became a shanty town, a local histo-rian describes it as similar to the Wild West. Houses were hastily thrown up without running water, sanitation or sewerage. A salesman travelling through was so shocked by the state of the town that, when he called at Birmingham, he left a sovereign with the Methodist missionaries to go and preach at Redditch.

The early history of the needle trade is one of constant battles between the needle makers and the needle masters. When a foot-operated stamping machine was introduced in 1830, the needlemakers assembled and marched to a factory and smashed the machines. They were on their way to a second factory when they were met by what they said was 'a ghost' and changed their minds. A needle pointer earned as much as £5 because, as he sharpened the needles, he inhaled the steel dust so that he rarely lived above the age of 30. Various inventions, such as a muzzle of magnets which trapped the steel dust, would have improved his life expectancy, but these were smashed up by the needle pointers as they didn't want to lose their high wages.

Spontaneous combustion

Abel Morrall has already been mentioned in the Alcester chapter, when his nephew was involved in the curious death of his wife. In 1898 Abel Morrall's factory moved from The Griffin Inn, Green Lane, Studley to a huge factory near Redditch railway station. It sold everything from buttons to zips but was famous for its Aero Cable and Knitting Pins.

Ghost stories from the needle factories are very rare and it's thanks to Sheila for this one:

I used to work at Abel Morrall's. The second block to their factory was down by the railway line where they made the AERO knitting needles. All kinds of strange things happened there. Each night, a security guard at had to go all round the build. One night he was, as usual, the only person in the building and as he walked round he noticed that a lady on the first floor had put a teddy by her typewriter. He went up on to the third floor and there was an identical teddy on the floor. He picked it up and thought nothing of it, but when he returned to the previous floor, the original teddy had disappeared.

In the building was a long, dark passage with an empty room at the end. The security guard always said he hated going along there, it sent the hairs on the back of his neck prickling. Occasionally, a police dog would need to go down or one of the staff called in with a dog, and no dog would ever go down that passageway, no matter how much you coaxed and pulled. Also, the guard said that he always felt inexplicably hot down there. In 1984 or 5 the block burned down.

117

The fire investigators said that it had started in a room at the end of the passageway, yet there was nothing in that room that could have started the fire. It was a complete mystery.

Ernie in Boomerang (01527 68250)

From the centre of the town, Mount Pleasant runs up a hill southwards. You once had to pay to walk along here as it was a toll road, the old pub known as The Gate Hangs Well is a reminder of those days.

A narrow road known as Beaufort Street is on the left. Until recently, 'Boomerang' was on this corner. The organisers accepted almost anything saleable and resold for charity. The premises were an old factory, Clifford Springs, and were originally built by the Tilley family as a bakery.

An imaginative reconstruction. Unfortunately Boomerang was closed at the time of going to press so the background of an antique shop was provided by Second Chance at St Andrew's Square, Droitwich.

Boomerang was supervised by Pauline, mother of five and an experienced charity-shop worker, assisted by young Stella.

We have all kinds of strange goings-on here. We call whatever-it-is 'Ernie'. If something happens, we shout 'Ernie, stop mucking about'. We hear so many strange bumps and bangs that we don't take any notice of them now. One of the most common is a rustling sound, like the swish of a silk skirt going past. We hear someone moving about upstairs with the books and clothes, but when we go up, no-one is there. Sometimes we go upstairs and find everything on the floor. We say to each other, 'How can this happen when no-one has been up here today?'.

Things disappear. I have lost two pairs of specs since I have been here. I know where I put them, they've just gone and I have never found them. We came in one morning and there was glass on the floor, a window had been broken from the inside in a little room that we keep locked all the time. Then we sometimes have a strong smell of disinfectant, like TCP. It's mainly in my office. You can walk in and out of the smell, it seems to be in a certain patch.

It's not only us, our customers often make a remark about something peculiar. A few days ago one of the customers went upstairs and felt a really cold breeze, she came shooting down the stairs.

We moved here during a cold spell in November 2006. The first thing that happened was in a little room at the back of the premises. In it was an old black leather chair, surrounded by brochures, catalogues and other information about Clifford Springs. While we were clearing the room and getting rid of everything, we both had an awful feeling that someone was there, watching us. It was as if somebody was there who didn't want you.

We set up our desk and two chairs in the middle of the shop next to the kitchen and we were absolutely freezing! We had only been here a few weeks when I saw a shadow move through the middle of the shop and out through a doorway. I said to Stella, 'Did someone just walk past?. Stella said that out of the corner of her eye, she had seen the dark shape of a person moving past. Although she hadn't seen any features or anything, she had the impression that it was male. It was quite scarey, we shot out of the shop. We have now moved our office to a small room on the right-hand side of the shop, where it's warmer.

We have a lot of problems with the telephone. We don't have trouble ringing out but people have trouble ringing in. They've tried to use it but it's not working, loads of customers can't get through. (The author tried to ring, the first time the line was silent, the second time there was a continuous dialling tone but she managed to get through on the third attempt). We have these massive phone bills showing that we have telephoned all kinds of places, Kent, Cardiff, Spain and even three telephone calls to Jamaica. Sometimes I phone some of the numbers listed to see who it is. One of the Jamaican numbers was to the police station! Why would I want to phone the Jamaican police? The people on the other end have no recollection of our having phoned them. We have to pay the bills as they are listed as coming from our line. I wondered if there was a crossed line outside or something.

In November a paranormal society, Parasearch, came to stay overnight on the premises. They brought various monitors with them and an unusually high level of electrical activity was recorded in the far right hand corner of the shop. Thinking about it, a lot of weird incidents have occurred here. Just before Christmas 2007, we had a disk jockey's desk there for about three weeks, together with a lot of old records, so we tried it out. We put on various records and we really enjoyed it. Our favourite was one particular forties compilation, but when it came to the song, 'I'll be loving you, always, it suddenly went 'whoosh' and became very loud. We thought somebody had turned it up so we rushed to the office door but nobody was there. We turned the record off and when we came back into the office Stella had a really creepy cold feeling all over. She felt as if somebody else was there.

A lot of strange things happen when we play music. The tapes go loud and soft and sometimes turn themselves off completely. The radio goes off by itself, we go and have a fiddle with it but we can't get it to work. Then an hour or two later, it will come on of its own accord. Our office is the other side of the wall of this electrically-charged corner. Against the wall is a TV and a shelf. Occasionally we have the TV on if the shop is quiet. It will be working perfectly normally, then it will suddenly start blaring out.

Articles jump off the shelf and land on the floor, unbroken. Not long after we moved in, a glass was on the shelf and the next minute it was on the floor. Three times last week a Boden cafetiere jumped off the shelf. You don't see it happen, but one minute it's on the shelf and the next second it's on the floor, unbroken. A few yards away is a closed circuit television on a shelf, that fell off for absolutely no reason.

Also against the wall of the corner is the downstairs loo. This is Stella's responsibility which brings her into the conversation:

The trouble we have with that downstairs loo is unbelievable. It will work properly for three or four months then it will be blocked for about three weeks. Nobody can use it, we put a big notice on it, Out of Order. We can't afford professional people so we have tried bicarbonate of soda and vinegar, drain unblockers, wire coat hangers, and I have even put my hand down it but I can't feel anything. Then suddenly after about three weeks, it will clear itself.

Similarly, the drain outside floods for no reason. It doesn't flood when it's pouring with rain, when you think it should flood. Again, I have put my hand down it and nothing is there. We have someone who comes into the shop who clears drains for a living. He says there's nothing wrong with it, there's no blockage. It will be blocked up for about two days and then it will be running perfectly.

Some of the thing that happen are really scarey. There are two sets of lights to be switched off when we leave, Pauline switches the one set off in the office, then we make our way through the shop and I switch the others off. We were crossing the office one evening in the semi-darkness when we heard a man laugh, 'He, he, he' just like that, very clearly.

When you are outside you can look at the building and check that all the lights are off but we sometimes have a call late at night from someone living nearby to tell us that the lights are on.

One morning, we had to go out of the shop to collect something. As we were going out, the radio went off and the noise of the traffic stopped. It was as if I was in an air bubble, as if time had stopped. I went cold from head to toe. We both shot out the front door then the radio came back on. It was the spookiest thing. Another morning we thought there was a gas leak. We both felt drained, sick and dizzy, then come lunchtime, we were both as right as rain.

Only last week, I was sitting in the office with a volunteer and a couple of yards away, in the office, was an ordinary folding plastic chair, folded up and leaning against the wall. We watched, open-mouthed as it slowly unfolded itself. It finished with a final quick 'whoosh' and a click.

Am I scared working here? Not really, I don't think whatever-it-is is particularly nasty. The only place where I'm afraid to go is in the little back room where we had that horrible sensation when we first moved in. It feels as if someone is watching you and waiting for you to turn your back so that he can do something terrible.

The final word comes from Pauline:

We have been here for a year now. We rarely get frightened, we just accept anything that happens. But we have given up telling people about it. Nobody will believe us. They just take the mickey out of us. They seem to think we are stupid or crazy.

We have a lot of house clearance stuff from people who have died. People become attached to their belongings, and I have sometimes wondered if their soul or spirit or whatever sometimes comes here with them.

Mount Pleasant – Night Riders

About 50 years ago Francis and her husband were living in a family house on Mount Pleasant, opposite the road known as 'The Mayfields'.

My husband and I slept in the front bedroom overlooking Mount Pleasant and my son was 16, he had the attic bedroom also overlook-

121

ing the road. In the early hours of one morning there was a terrific din coming in from the road outside, it woke us up. It was the noise of horses, I should say about four of them, galloping. No jangling of chains or anything, just horses. My husband jumped out of bed and looked out of the window. It was winter-time and dark but in those days, Mount Pleasant was the main road through the town and so it was well lit. He said, 'There's nothing there'. I had a look too but I couldn't see anything. The next morning, my son said he had heard it as well and had looked out of the window but nothing was there.

Over the next few weeks we heard the same noise three times. We all heard it, all three of us and we all looked out but none of us saw anything. It seemed to start at the Park Inn, go past our house and down the hill. It went on for quite a few minutes. Another funny thing was that they never came back, they always went the one way.

This is not the first time phantom horses have been heard going along Mount Pleasant. In 1946, a young man, Donald Reynolds, lived in Wythall and had a slow puncture on his motor bike. He thought he would test the repair by riding into Redditch for a shandy then on to Headless Cross. He invited a friend to go with him. Mount Pleasant is a long slow climb so they got off their motor bikes and pushed them up the last bit. By that time it was dark. They heard the noise of horses approaching, so they drew their bikes to one side. First they saw swivelling lights, then they saw a set of wheels and a coach came rushing past them. It looked quite real except that the driver had no head. The coach swept past and disappeared. Donald was so terrified he slept with his bedroom light on for the next few weeks and never went near Headless Cross again.

Headless Cross – The curious tale of the Chesterfield

Halfway between Crabbs Cross and Redditch is Headless Cross. This is one of the highest points of Redditch and the Victorian water tower is a splendid landmark.

People wonder if there is something sinister here because of its name but, the name probably comes from a Saxon chief, Hedda, who once lived here. Headless Cross used to be famous for its thirteen pubs. A tiny area on the Bromsgrove side of Headless Cross was known as Nailpasser Green as the nailers used to walk from Bromsgrove to sample the ample beer here.

Although Headless Cross was first mentioned in 1275 most of the houses are Victorian, built to serve the workers of local factories. The sumptuous red-leather Chesterfield settee mentioned below, could be the same age as the Victorian house, as 'The Couch' was designed many years ago by one of the Earls of Chesterfield (now an obsolete title) in the 1800s. The owner of the Chesterfield says:

This is an old house in Headless Cross. I have been trying to find out how old it is, I know it's Victorian but I don't have a precise date. It's my husband's house and I moved in about two-and-a-half years ago. Sometime after I had moved in, his father passed away and my husband was trying to get rid of his furniture so we ended up with this old dark red leather settee, with the buttons. After that, ghostly things started going on.

In the evening, after tea, I can hear children playing up and down the stairs and giggling. I don't see anything, just hear them. My husband can't hear anything, he's not a bit sensitive. When I come home from work, I always tap on the window and look in to see if my daughter's here. I looked through the window one afternoon to see someone getting up off the settee. You know how older people get up off a low settee differently to younger people, and I could tell that she was quite elderly by the way that she was pushing herself up by the arm. She was wearing a blue and white striped jumper. I came in expecting to see somebody but no-one was there. A few weeks later we were going through some old photographs that I have never seen before and among them was a picture of a woman. It was the woman I had seen, even down to the blue and white striped jumper. She was holding my husband's hand, he was a little boy, and it turned out that she was his mother. I have seen her three or four times. My husband is subject to bouts of depression and she appears whenever he's down, although he doesn't see her, but I do. Every time I see her she's getting up off the settee.

Then I've seen another woman here. I haven't a clue who this one is. One evening, I fell asleep on the settee. You know that sometimes

A lady in Headless Cross inherited a Chesterfield complete with mother-in-law!

you can feel that someone is looking at you, this feeling was so strong that it woke me up and there was a lady peering down at me. She was dressed in white layers and she had the 1920s-type bobbed hair, curling under her chin. She was leaning over me, staring. She just went.

Crabbs Cross – Conferring with the dead

Almost three miles out of town is Crabbs Cross island where roads leave for Bromsgrove, Redditch, Birmingham, Stratford and Evesham. Charles I is said to have reviewed his troops at this spot in about 1642. Two counties, Worcestershire and Warwickshire, meet here which made it very popular for the illegal sport of bare-fist boxing in the 1800s, because if the magistrate arrived from one county to arrest those involved, the pugilists only had to step a few feet into the next county and they were out of their jurisdiction.

Some of the houses in Crabbs Cross houses go back to the early 1800s. Janice's* friend became the proud owner of one of them:

One of our circle of friends inherited a large run-down house from his father. When I say 'run-down', I'm not exaggerating. It was in a terrible condition. The mess it was in had to be seen to be believed. The rubbish was piled high each side of the rooms leaving a narrow gangway to walk through. We had to hire at least six skips.

In all the chaos, it was necessary to find the deeds. I stood in the living room and concentrated. It came to me that there was something about a large cupboard against the wall in front of me. I'm not in the habit of looking through people's cupboards but my friend was keen that I should have a go. The cupboard was full of records, books, oil cans and beer mats but there, at the very back, was a large brown envelope. We had found the first deed.

Now we needed the second deed. By the door was a large window and beneath it, loaded with rubbish, was a settee. I knew there was something about that sofa but it was coming up to five o'clock in the evening when we needed to disperse and go back to our homes. We met up again a couple of days later and the first thing we did was to turn the settee upside down, partly because of my hunch and partly to tip all the junk out. There was the second deed.

I often think about it and wonder why I was able to do this.

Plymouth Road – The Gardener

Plymouth Road runs from Mount Pleasant to the railway station. On the left is the old cemetery and Elizabeth lives nearby:

People say to me, 'Fancy living near a cemetery' but I find it a lovely tranquil place.

In the 1960s I was living further up Plymouth Road than I do now, and behind us were some allotments. They have now been built over. A little path ran alongside our garden on to the allotments and my father could take a short cut up to the Evesham Road along this path.

There was a gardener on the allotments, I think he was employed by the Council to keep them tidy. His name was Joe, we all called him Joe the Gardener, he was a stocky little man with a cloth cap and he carried a long bill-posters rake with him that was worn out. I think he used to rake the rubbish up with it for burning.

I was about six or seven at the time, and my mother sent me on an errand to get something from Oakley Road. When I came back I gave my mother what she wanted and I said, 'Oh, by the way I've just seen Joe the gardener again'. My mother said, 'You can't have, don't tell lies'. Evidently he had died a week or two before.

Muskett's Wood – A final joke

Musketts Wood has now disappeared from our maps. The name has been reduced to a footpath, Musketts Way, dividing Pitcher Oak Wood from the golf course.

Eddie Smith has just published his memoirs in a booklet currently available in all good bookshops. He was found as a little black baby on a Redditch doorstep, was adopted and rose to become quite prominent in the town. He only discovered in recent years that he was swapped at birth for another illegitimate baby as his mother wanted a baby girl, so he became, as he says, 'surplus to requirements'.

Eddie doesn't mention the ghost story in his memoirs but he tells it here:

I have only ever seen what could have been a ghost once.

When I was in my early twenties, I used to hang out with a group of young lads. There were five of us and we were all mates. We lived in Lodgings in Birchfield Road about one-and-a-half miles (about 2.5 km) west of Redditch town centre. We used to work for local contractors until we came to the point where we had used up our tax allowance, then we would claim our paid tax back and go off on our travels. That day, we had got to the point where we had just left work, we had given in our notices and were off to celebrate at the local pub. To reach the pub we had to go through Muskett's Wood on the outskirts of the town. It was a nice evening walk and we were all chatting and joking.

When we got close to the golf course, it got a bit misty. We saw this person walking towards us so the group parted and we let him through, not taking very much notice of him. Then somebody said, 'Didn't somebody just go through us?'. We said 'Yes', and he said, 'Where is he then?'. We looked round and he had completely disappeared.

I remember him very clearly because he looked just like Eric Morecombe. He was in his fifties, about six feet tall, thin with glasses and he combed his hair over exactly in the same way that Eric Morecambe did.

Saint George's - Its curious history

Saint George's is right next to the large island where the Alvechurch Highway and Coventry Highway intersect, yet it's curiously isolated in a quiet corner, with a church and a patch of green. The story goes that the church was built here in 1875 because nearby, in Grange Road, was an old factory that was being used as a workhouse. If you were in the workhouse then you had to go to church so the upright citizens of St Stephens in the centre of Redditch were joined every Sunday morning by a crowd of down-and-outs. They were not happy about this. It so happened that a local needle manufacturer, Mr Milward, wanted to build a church which would not only give him some heavenly pips but where he would be of great importance. So it was agreed that Saint George's would be built which was near to the workhouse and the misfits could attend there each Sunday. Mr Milward gave half the funding and the vicar of St Stephen's was so glad to get rid of them that he gave the other half.

At first there was no vicarage and the incumbent lived in a house rented from the Miss Smith's, who owned a local factory. However, one of the Miss Smith's took a liking to the Rev Michelle, the vicar in the 1930's, and he could not get rid of her. He wrote to the bishop saying 'You must get me away from this woman' with the result that the vicarage was built.

Incidentally, St George's has the best organ in Worcestershire except for the one in the Cathedral. It came from Queen's College, Oxford .

St George's is said to be haunted. White ladies have been seen going through its doors and some choirboys saw a misty face hanging on its walls. St George's has the best organ in Worcestershire except for the Cathedral. A local organist, Philip Jarvis, says that while he is playing the organ, he can hear someone open the main doors and come in but when he goes to see who it is, no-one is there. Both the next two narratives are from houses near St George's church.

St George's Church in the winter sunshine.

The Cluedo Menace

Julie moved into a house in St George's about ten years ago, and over the last few years strange things have happened. She says:

I have been able to accept it until now but just recently they have been quite frightening.

I dropped my daughter at college, came in and did the housework and vacuumed round. Then I went upstairs to go into the bathroom. When I came downstairs, three Cluedo pieces had been carefully arranged on the bottom step but one, in a 'U' shape. It was the way they were arranged that got me. I had walked upstairs only thirty seconds before and the front door had been locked, I'm very fussy about that. It's not even a game that we have in the house. That freaked me out. I took them to my next door neighbour and she put the three pieces on the fire and burned them.

Since then, I keep getting one piece in all sorts of strange places like the bottom of my suitcase.

I have had other experiences. I have seen my dad at the bottom of my bed, my daughter has seen him as well. Other people that I don't know have been sitting on the bed. I see them when I wake up at night.

My daughter is at college and she's so terrified that she sleeps with me in my room. Have you ever heard of a seventeen-year old sleeping with her mum?

My boyfriend sometimes comes round and he has a Border Collie. The dog went upstairs and started scratching on the door of my daughter's bedroom. He started barking howling and crying and his hackles rose. Usually, the dog would run in the house quite happily but this time he wouldn't go near my daughter. He went into my room and was sick all over my bed.

Five minutes later I went into the bathroom and said to my daughter, 'Can you smell that funny smell?'. It was as if someone had lit a match. She said, 'I noticed it when I went in earlier'. I walked into her bedroom to switch her tv off and I felt someone stroking the top of my head.

When my daughter was small, she was asleep upstairs and suddenly there was a big bang. My friend was here, we both ran upstairs. We went into my daughter's bedroom and her CD flew across the room from one side to the other. Also, there was that same smell that I have already in the bathroom.

I'm very fussy about switching lights off. I went out one day last week and when I came back, my daughter said, 'Why did you leave the lights on?' Another day I got home and the lights were on again and I know without a doubt that I switched them off.

The Housing Association have arranged for a representative to call from Stratford

The haunted digger

An intriguing anecdote was told at a meeting in the Palace Theatre in May 2008.

When I was about fourteen, and I'm now retired, the field at the back of St George's Church was our playground. We always called it Smith's Field, and the Council used it as a tip. One of the schools have it now. We used to play football there and generally mess about. On one side of the field was a sharp drop.

Two or three of us were down there one evening, it was nearly dark and the moon was up. The Council had left a large machine at the tip, I think it was a digger. As far as I know, we were the only ones in the field. Suddenly, the digger started up all of its own accord. I can hear it now. It had no lights on, but it slowly started going round the edge of the field. Remember, there was a sharp drop one side of the field and the digger went along right on the edge of the drop. I don't believe in ghosts and I'm not saying that no-one was driving it, but if there was someone, he was damn good, he only had the light of the moon to drive by and he went all along the edge of that embankment.

We all saw it go slowly round the edge of the field then stop where it started from. We watched it, gobsmacked, and we didn't see anyone get out of the cab.

BEOLEY – Apparition at the cross roads

Beoley lies to the north east of Worcestershire, not far from the Roman Icknield Stereet, the A435. The local historian reckons that Beoley was the motorway café for the Romans. A village once clustered round the old church but has now moved away to Holt End, leaving an area of green fields and scattered farms. In the church are the luxurious tombs of the Sheldons, dating back to the 1600s. William Sheldon founded the first English tapestry workshops.

In the 1850s, the vicar decided to raise money by conducting tours of the Sheldon vaults and after that he was so certain that he was being haunted by one of the Sheldons that he paid for a man to sleep at the foot of his bed.

Beoley Church stands isolated, its village has moved to Holt End.

Beoley was once on the main route from Redditch to Birmingham and the cross roads seem to attract all kinds of apparitions. Here are just a few of the many sightings:

A local resident was just travelling away from the crossroads late one evening in the 1950s when she saw a man in the road waving his arm frantically up and down. She thought her boyfriend was going to hit him and shouted at him to stop. The boyfriend hadn't seen anything but he jammed on his brakes. The man gave a gigantic leap into the hedge and disappeared.

Two young ladies, Rowena and Pauline, were going to the Village Inn at Holt End in 1972 for an evening out, and Rowena was driving. As they were going towards the cross roads they both saw a man in a deerstalker hat and a shoulder-length cape in the middle of the road. He suddenly vanished.

Tony O'Neill was driving with his wife through the crossroads in 1986 when they both saw a thin male, six feet tall, in a dark grey cagoule or trench coat which reached the floor. He had a small grey and white dog with him on a lead. Tony was about to overtake when, says Tony, 'Pop' and he disappeared like a bubble.

In 1988, Clint Longmuir had just reached the bottom of the hill at the cross roads late one evening when his headlights picked out the shape of a man on his left. Clint turned his head away for a second and when he looked back the man had gone.

In 1991 Andrew Proctor had not long passed his driving test and had turned into the cross roads ready to go up the hill. Suddenly a man appeared from nowhere and walked into the front of his car. He was tall, about fifty-ish and wearing a long black cloak with a hood. As Andrew drove past, he disappeared.

Moses Shrimpton rides again

Yet another Beoley anecdote was told at Studley Car Boot:

I was driving home to Holt End from Birmingham and I was just going past Beoley Church, going over the hill, when a man with a bike walked across the road in front of me. I banged on the brakes. My wife said, 'Have we hit him?'. We got out of the car and looked round, we couldn't see him anywhere. My wife said, 'Did he fall?'. I said, 'We must be seeing things'. We had both seen him. Then I remembered that there had been no bang as we hit him.

Further down the hill I noticed a police car. It turned out to be a police-dog handler, he had stopped to pick up an injured bird. We

130

Moses Shrimpton (drawing courtesy Alan Foxall)

started chatting, I said, 'I have just had a funny experience. I thought I had hit a man on a bike'. He told me a lot of people had seen him, it was the last person to be hung in Redditch and he's usually seen pushing his bike up the hill.

This is a reference to the murder of PC Davies by Moses Shrimpton in 1885. PC Davies was on his rounds in the early hours of the morning when he came across Moses, a well-known thief, who had stolen some chickens from a local farm. There was a fight and PC Davies was stabbed to death. A stone reading JD 1885 marks the spot where he was killed on the old Icknield Street, about half a mile from Weatheroak. Moses had been living in Redditch but had recently moved to Birmingham where he was known to the local police and was soon picked up.

The bicycle is an interesting feature. Nowhere in any of the newspaper reports, is a bicycle mentioned. 1885 is early for a two-wheeled bicycle but he could have had one of the old boneshakers.

A tribute to the fallen

Vanche Lanover Slade had been head choirboy at Beoley Church. He met a tragic death at Paschendale on 14th October 1917 when, at the age of 36, he died of his wounds. A plaque in Beoley Church bears his name.

A relative of his, Ian Sargeant, says:

My brother-in-law is in the army and he's based in Germany. I went over to see him with my wife and my two sons, aged five and one. We were passing where the battle took place and decided to visit the main cemetery. It was a hospital clearing station and it now has 10,500 graves. In the gatehouse are books with names and a reference by them so that you can find the grave that you want. Vanche's name was listed but there was no reference number. We decided to just have a walk round in the cemetery. We began to walk up the centre and that very minute my five year old son ran off one side and went straight to the grave. He shouted out 'What was his name?' (he could read at five). I couldn't believe it. Goosepimples went all up my arms.

The charcoal burner

Beoley is such a beautiful spot that a young man, Anthony, brought his new wife here.

131

I got married for a second time and I went with my new wife and youngest son for a picnic up Beoley Hill, near Redditch. There's a wooded area in the fields on the opposite side of the road to the church, with a dip in the middle. I couldn't stay there, I could hear crackling noises all round me like a bush burning. I thought there was a fire in the wood and looked for the smoke and flames but there weren't any. I was surrounded by the noise and it was quite loud. My wife and son couldn't hear the noise, but it quite unnerved me. When I got out of the wood I couldn't hear a thing.

Close to St Leonard's church is a small hill known as 'The Mount', which has never been excavated but may possibly be an Iron Age (600BC to 400AD) hill fort. Did Anthony tune into a skirmish taking place two thousand or so years ago? There's also an old story that a charcoal burner fell asleep and was burned to death on Beoley Hill and you can still hear his screams and the crackling of his fire when the wind is high at night.

13. REDDITCH NEW TOWN

n the early 1960s the Minister of Housing and Local Government wanted to start clearing the Birmingham city's slums, but there was a shortage of land. Redditch was therefore designated as a new town in 1963, to take the Birmingham overspill. The population of Redditch was then 32,000 but it was planned to rise to 70,000 by 1980 (it has now remained fairly stable at about 80,000). During its lifetime the Redditch Development Corporation built about 15,000 homes, 111 miles of new roads, 19 miles of sewers, 37 local shops, 20 schools and 750,000 square feet of shopping space, among them the Kingfisher Shopping Centre. It was named after the boat sponsored by Redditch during World War II.

When the Kingfisher Shopping Centre was in the process of being built, the workmen were plagued by strange events. Lifts would whizz up and down in the night, a children's carousel in the centre started up on its own in the early hours of the morning, people were seen in places where access was impossible and the police were called out several times because security guards heard a child crying but there was never any child. The security guards had to clock in at certain points and one night, a guard was walking across a balcony outside (what is now) Primark's, when, to his horror, he saw 'a guy in a robe-shaped thing' gliding rapidly towards him. He rushed into the lift, closed the doors and breathed a sigh of relief as the lift began to descend but when he looked up into the mirrors round the edge of the lift, he saw the ghost was in the lift with him. Fortunately, as the lift descended, it left the ghost behind.

A congregational church and cemetery had to be demolished to make way for the centre and many residents suggest that this is the reason for the strange incidents, however, curious things happened throughout the centre and not just in that area.

Whatever-it-was has now calmed down and although shop assistants report the occasional strange experience, this is no more than in any other shopping centre.

The poltergeist

The following incidents occurred in a large central store in the summer of 2008. The staff were reorganising the store to make way for a new department, and the upper floor was empty, except for some rubbish bins.

The Kingfisher Centre in its early days.

The manageress went to empty some rubbish, then she said to me, 'Did you follow me downstairs?'. As she went back down, she heard footsteps behind her but when she turned round, no-one was there.

The staff were sitting in the staff room when the kettle turned itself on.

To save electricity, all the lights in the building are fitted with sensors and only come on when someone walks into the room. The manageress arrived this morning and the light of the upstairs floor was on. She was the first to arrive and no-one was there.

The following disturbances are from another store and occurred over the Christmas period of 2008:

I was serving a customer last week when a felt tip pen flew off the counter. There were no staff by the pen or in that area. I had my back to it but the customer I was serving saw it, and I heard it land on the floor with a loud bang.

I went into one of the ladies' toilets and just as I closed the door behind me, I saw a shadow going past the toilet door. I sat down on the toilet and saw the shadow go past the other way. There was no-one in the ladies room with me and there were no footsteps as the shadows passed.

One of the staff members has seen a little girl following one of the managers around upstairs in the stockroom. The little girl has long curly blonde hair and is wearing a red coat. She appeared so real the member of staff asked the manager if she was her little girl.

Gee whizz!

There are many curious tales about the lifts in car park 3. For example, two ladies from a nearby office followed a lady into the lift but when they closed the doors, they were the only two in the lift! This one is from a young mum, Stella.

Mum and I decided to go shopping in the Kingfisher Centre, taking my toddler with us.

Mum had had a knee operation so we used the disability car park where she could have free use of a wheelchair. There was nowhere to park on the ground floor next to the office giving out the wheelchairs, so I dropped mum off and went on to park. The car park was packed so I had to go right up to level five with the car before I found a space.

My toddler was in a pushchair so I needed to use the lift to go down. I pressed the call button but the lift went whizzing up and down and didn't stop at my floor. I was just wondering how I was going to get down all those stairs with a pushchair when it eventually stopped. I went to get in but the doors closed before I was in properly. Anyone who has used this lift will tell you that it's normally very slow-moving. I pushed the button to go down and instead the lift went up. I thought somebody was larking about so, when the lift stopped on the top floor, I shot out to have a word with them but nobody was there. Finally, I made it to the ground floor but as the doors opened they made a terrible grating noise. I was glad to get out as the lift gave me a creepy feeling.

NEW TOWN VILLAGES

The following villages were created by the Redditch Development Corporation. Each satellite village had a grocery store, post office, hairdressers, pub etcetera so that residents could live there quite happily without having to go into the town centre. They were situated in natural hollows so that a view across Redditch would be one of green foliage and the town was designed so that everyone had access to the open countryside.

The villages are listed from north to the south through the suburbs:

Church Hill - Flying home

The old Roman Icknield Street passes through Church Hill and has been preserved by a footpath. The next strange experience is told by Irene, she and her neighbour live about 250 yards (228m) west of the footpath. The old mill pond is just off the A4023.

My neighbour is a lovely chap, always ready to help. My conifer was growing very tall so he came and cut it for me and wouldn't accept any payment. If he doesn't see me around he knocks on the door to make sure I'm OK.

Not far from our house is an old mill pond and he takes his dog for a walk there most days. You have to walk through a gap in the hedge to get to the pond, and, recently, after he walked through he saw a chap in air force uniform, with wings on his shoulders, standing on one of the wooden platforms overlooking the pond, put there for the fishermen. It was raining cats and dogs but this chap was standing there looking as smart as anything. There was a crease in his trousers and his shoes were shining.

My neighbour is a friendly type so he said, 'Good morning' but the man didn't reply and just went on staring at the water. My neighbour walked past for about twenty yards, then he thought, 'I wonder if he's alright, I'd better go and see' and he turned back, but the man had gone.

From there you can see in every direction. The man must have really sprinted to get out of sight so quickly. There were trees about but it was winter and you could see though the branches.

Lodge Park - A new house - with an occupant

About 25 years ago, Clifford and his wife bought a 30-year old house in Lodge Park. Clifford explains why they resold it before they had moved in!

When we were clearing the house out before we moved in, my wife saw the ghost of a man with a flat cap. We went back home and she started crying. She said, 'I don't want to move to that house, I have seen a ghost'. I said, 'Don't worry, we'll put it back on the market'.

When we went to see the solicitor and said we wanted to cancel the sale, he asked, 'Why?' and I explained about the ghost. He said that he wasn't at all surprised, it happened quite often with various properties. Anyway, we sold the house and just before the buyers were about to move in they themselves cancelled the sale without any explanation.

Eventually we sold it. A little while after, we saw the neighbour

An imaginative re-consruction of the deceased builder in the new house.

of the property where my wife had seen the ghost. She told us, 'I was living here when that house was built. Two workmen were working there, they had their lunch time and when they came back they had had too much to drink. There was a fight, one of them was knocked down and he eventually died.' She described the workman and it exactly matched the description of the ghost my wife had seen.

(His wife was listening to the conversation and adds) I can still see him in my mind's eye. He was a small man, small built and slim. It was the flat cap that stands out in my memory. He was about 45, he was wearing a shirt and trousers and the shirt was blue. He looked just like a general builder.

Greenlands – The punk

Greenlands has a large playing field with various facilities and this mum was probably collecting her son from there.

I had collected my son from Greenlands and was driving home to-wards the Redditch centre. It was about 6.30 at night, another half hour and it would have been dark so it must have been September or October. To get on to the Warwick Highway from Greenlands there's a slip road. I was at the bottom of the slip road when I saw a man behaving very strangely on the side of the road a few yards in front, he was moving very quickly and he went straight into the road without looking. I said to my son, 'Just look at him, he must be mad!'. My son was nine years old at the time, he said he couldn't see anyone.

The man was tall and slim with black hair in a modern style, mostly on end. He was wearing modern jeans and a hooded top. Then he just completely disappeared. I couldn't believe it. As I drove past I looked to see if anything had happened to him but nothing was there.

Woodrow - Broad Oak and its entities

Most of these satellite villages were built on farmland and some of them, such as Woodrow, take their name from the farm. The next two stories are both from Woodrow.

Barbara's grandparents lived in a house known as, 'Broad Oak'. She says that it was near what is now the Woodrow Centre, on top of a rise.

In those days, it was surrounded by countryside and a narrow road led up to it. I used to enjoy freewheeling down the hill. It was a lovely modern house with four bedrooms, two reception, a kitchen and a big wide staircase, French doors and a balcony. It was a beautiful place, built after the war and very modern but it never had electricity connected. It had a generator in the garage. The generator would be charged during the day and at night, if there were a lot of lights on and they were using a lot of electricity, the lights would go dim. It was very eerie.

I never liked going there. It felt weird to me. Many strange things happened there.

Things used to move and disappear. I put some money on a shelf, then £1 was missing. By the next morning, it had come back. Then they had a self-assembly pack arrive. The screws were not in the packing so they left it until the morning and then there they were.

They had a lot of antiques, and things were sometimes found smashed on the floor. The son's wife lived there and they were always accusing her of breaking things that she swore she hadn't done. One night there was a noise as if someone was throwing a basket of apples down the stairs. They all rushed out but nothing was there. Then there was a strange smell in the hallway, a very strong odour. Someone remarked that it smelt like the stuff they put in coffins. They had a little office there with a telephone. The telephone rang, I went in to answer it and the door slammed itself shut. I couldn't open it. It was quite frightening.

They had a black Alsation dog and while they were there the dog used to howl for no reason.

It was demolished by the new town development and flats were built on the site, they were only small flats, the blocks were about three stories high. My grandparents moved to Easemore Road and were very happy there, they had nothing strange happening.

Before I retired, I was a social worker. I went to see a lady in a certain flat who was telling me she had awful trouble. Other people in the flats had seen things moving and had seen ghostly people – everyone was quite excited about it. I looked out of the window and I said to her, 'I'm sure these flats are built on the site of Broad Oak. I always thought that it was haunted'. They had so many problems there that the Church had to come and exorcise the block.

Woodrow – Who are you?

Peter* went to live in Woodrow in about 1985, the house had just been refurbished.

When I was in bed at night I used to see a strange light through the glass panel over the bedroom door, although no lights were on in the house. It was a weird light, but I used to ignore it. As time went on I kept seeing this strange light.

One morning, I got up for work at 7am when it was still dark. I made a beeline for the WC opposite the bedroom. 1 had seen this strange light again through the glass panel, and I thought now I can see what it really is. I got out of the bedroom and I still had my hand on the bedroom door when I saw the glow on the stairwell. Then, a few yards away, in the pitch black on the stairwell, I saw a woman's face. Being the inquisitive type, I got up close, and there I saw the apparition of a woman in midair in the stairwell. She was walking, but kept on the same spot. She was elderly, with long hair and she was wearing a white gown from her chin to her feet, which were bare. I could see through her, and in a cupboard behind her was a bright light. I stood looking at the woman and she turned round and looked at me. I watched her and she watched me for about ten minutes or so

I couldn't get over it I thought this is incredible. Then I had to go because I would have been late for work.

A couple of years later my son wanted me to wake him up early

139

An imaginative reconstruction of the lady hanging in the stairwell.

for work. This time, when I got on to the landing and looked towards the window I could see two great circular glowing white orbs, each about the size of a football. They were chasing each other, almost touching each other then moving about a metre away and coming together again. I was standing at the top of the stairs watching this for several minutes. Again, I was amazed. I had to leave it and go into my son's room or he would have been late for work. I have not seen anything like that before or since.

I was asleep in bed when I heard someone calling my name and telling me to get up. I was annoyed for a bit then eventually I woke up to find no-one there. I looked at the clock and discovered that I had overslept. If I hadn't been woken up, I would have been late for work.

Once, I was asleep and dreamed that a woman was pulling my arm telling me to follow her. She kept pulling and pulling until I woke up. Then, when I opened my eyes, I saw her disappear through the wall.

I'm now working nights and sleeping during the day. Last year, I happened to wake up and as my eyes got accustomed to the light, I saw a woman standing in the doorway of the bedroom. It gave me a bit of a fright. She was middle-aged and wearing strange clothes, an old-fashioned flowery dress and longish hair, She was standing still and staring at me. I made a movement and she disappeared through the door, which was closed.

When my wife came in I asked her if she had come into my bedroom but she said she had been out all morning.

140

Winyates East – Harry Potter pays a visit

In the middle of June 2008, the author met a sixteen-year old at Studley Car Boot who didn't want to be named but said that she lived in Winyates East where all kinds of strange things happened:

When we first moved in I was about eleven and my brother was fourteen. About that time the Harry Potter video first came out. We were sitting there, watching Harry Potter, when the video started playing backwards and a glass flew off the shelf and hit the window.

Upstairs in my bedroom was a clown money box where you had to take the head off to get the money out. As I entered the room, the head of the clown moved and turned towards me.

Things often disappeared. Mum's friend was helping her to decorate, she was downstairs on a ladder, she put the paintbrush down and the next second it had gone. It reappeared upstairs in my brother's bedroom. Most things seemed to happen round my brother's bedroom.

Another time I was playing with a Ouija board with two friends and one of them let go of the glass, which apparently you're not supposed to do. Immediately loud banging came from my brother's bedroom upstairs. He had stopped the night at his best friend's house, so he wasn't there. My best friend stopped the night at my house and every time we tried to go to sleep, a loud banging came from my brother's room. It was a sort of thudding noise, as if something had been dropped. We turned off the electrics in case it was something to do with that but the banging went on.

We were playing with the Ouija board one night and we freaked out. My brother wasn't playing, he was sitting watching, and the glass spelt out everything that he had in his head. He thought of his birthday and the glass spelt that out, then the date of his grandad's death – nobody else knew that, only him, then the pin number of his bank card.

My brother always wore a cross but he took it off one night. When he woke up in the morning here were scratches across his stomach as if someone had tried to scratch him.

Somewhere in Redditch – another doggie story

Our Jack Russell bitch used to walk round and round her basket, pushing her blanket round with her nose to make her bed. The basket used to creak and groan. She did this every evening at her bedtime between nine and ten. The blanket was always kept in the kitchen.

She had to be put down at the age of thirteen because of ill-health and old age. About three months later, my husband and I were sitting in the living room and we heard the same noise coming from the kitchen. We looked at each other and he said, 'We haven't got a dog, have we?'. I said, 'No'.

Neither of us went to investigate. We just sat there.

The fisherman's tale

Twice a year, a Vintage Fishing Tackle fair is held at The Abbey Stadium near the centre of Redditch. The next story was told by Martin at the November 2008 Fair:

I had an extremely interesting experience about two-and-a-half years ago when I was working at Barrington in Oxford.

We were doing a refurbishment job on a house built in 1751. I'm a carpenter and there was a whole team, about five of us, electrician, plumber, plasterer and so on. I was there for two months.

All sorts of strange things happened. It was mostly the noises. You would hear footsteps overhead. I would say to my mate, 'Who's that upstairs?'. He would say, 'Nobody'. I would say, 'Somebody has just walked across upstairs'. This happened every two or three days.

Things moved. We had a dust sheet laid out downstairs and a brick holding it down. The brick would roll off of its own accord. We had a small table with our tea-making stuff on it. The teaspoon was always on the floor. It first we thought it was just clumsy workmen but it happened too often for that.

The people who had just moved in were frightened by it and wanted to sell the house and move out straight away. We said to them 'You can't do that, we've been here for two months and we've put up with it'.

I didn't believe in ghosts when I started working there and I still don't but I must say it was very suspicious.

14. THE STOURPORT-on-SEVERN AREA

ew towns are usually considered to be a product of the twentieth century but in 1770s, an entirely new town was built on a sandy waste by the river Severn. Even the name was new. Previously the waste had been known as Lower Mitton but then it was known as Stourport-on-Severn. The inspiration for the town came from the Earl of Bridgewater. He wanted to link the two main rivers in England, the Severn and the Thames, with the Worcester and Birmingham canal. James Brindley was already working for the Earl and was therefore chosen as the architect of his plan. The river Severn needed to join the canal at some point, and Brindley chose Lower Mitton. To raise funds, the Earl lived very frugally, with few, if any staff, and eating simple food and rarely entertaining. Unfortunately, Brindley died before his new town was completed. Many of the early basins and locks are still in existence.

Although Lower Mitton was a sandy waste, the area is rich in history. On the other side of the river are the Redstone caves, where a great hermitage once clung to the cliffs. The river could be forded here at low tide and it was a popular route from Worcester to Wales. The funeral cortege of Henry VIII's elder brother, Prince Arthur, probably came this way on its way back from Ludlow in 1502. Across the river and overlooking the town is the church of Areley Kings. The medieval poet, Layamon, was priest here in about 1200 and this is where he wrote his Brut, a chronicle on the history of Britain, thus preserving the tales of King Arthur and his knights. It was also the first work in Middle English.

Until the Beeching Act closed the railways in the 1960s, Stourport-on-Severn was the great holiday town of the Midlands with hundreds of folk streaming down the hill from the station each bank holiday to enjoy themselves on the boats, steamers and playgrounds or simply to walk along the river bank. There are still several caravan parks, a static fairground, an amusement park and several fish-and-chip shops.

The centre of the town was developed in the late 1700s on a 200 year lease with the result that suddenly, in the 1990s, owners of much of the property in the town discovered that the ground on which they stood did not belong to them. Some businesses had to close and among the casualties was the Methodist church which was one of the oldest in the county and where John Wesley himself preached. The owners wanted to sell the building and the Methodists had to leave. Fortunately, a buyer was never found and after three years of frantic fund-raising the Methodists managed to raise the funds to purchase a new lease.

The magnificent Tontine

When the canal was first built, the directors and staff of the Staffordshire and Worcestershire canal company needed headquarters and it was decided to build a magnificent 100-bedroom hotel overlooking the river and use part of it as their base. The hotel eventually became known as the Tontine, named after an early form of life insurance in which a group of people would take out a policy where only the last surviving member would get the payout! This type of life insurance was made illegal for obvious reasons.

With the arrival of the railways, the fortunes of the canal company waned and the Tontine became a white elephant. Plans to demolish it in 1977 were, fortunately, abandoned and this prestigious contribution to Stourport history has been boarded up ever since.

One of Stourport's elderly widows, Marilyn, says that her husband, Martyn, used to go out every Saturday night for a drink, and she continues:

He was a friendly chap who liked talking to people, every Tom, Dick and Harry, so he heard all the local ghost stories. Several people told him that they had seen the ghost on the top floor of the Tontine looking out through the windows. She has curly fair hair, long flowing clothes and she usually wears a hat, possibly Edwardian. Two ghosts have also been seen in the bar area.

The Tontine in its hey-day.

144

The white lady of The Black Star

One of the oldest pubs in Stourport is the Black Star. Michelle is the Premises Licence Holder, her 'sidekick', Jack, is the licensee and her two daughters, Jasmine and Beth, help in the pub, assisted by Mick, the resident bar-tender. Although she only took over the pub a few years ago, her family has been in the licensing business as far back as she can remember.

Her great grandfather, John H Blackford (known as Jack) was so well-known and respected that he was given half a column in the Worcestershire newspapers when he died. He was a timber feller working across the Midlands and was a member of the Midland Counties Benefit Society and the Black Star Sick and Dividend Society. Tactfully, the press omitted to say that he died after he staggered out from the Black Star so intoxicated that he fell into a ditch and died from hypothermia.

As for the history of the Black Cross itself, the Stourport Civic Society has been working on the history of all the public houses in Stourport, and has discovered that the pub is traceable back to 1780, when the Rates Levy book has an entry for 'The Star' - its original name. The present public house is a combination of three buildings. The front section, nearest the street and now The Bar, is the original pub. The middle section, now the Lounge, may have been a chapel before it became Mitton House. The end section, now the kitchen and various etceteras was probably a school for the Waterways children with separate entrances for boys and girls. The land around the Black Star belonged to a farm but the farmhouse was demolished in the 1930s.

Michelle says:

I have been told that The Bar is the oldest part and could date back to the 17th century. In the attic above The Lounge you can still see the old church beams with carved stone lintels. On one is carved the date 1883 and EH, the initials of the licensee at that time, Eli Hitchon. I have also been told that during the war, part of the pub was used as a mortuary.

When I first came I walked through the main door and immediately noticed how very cold it was, and unsettling. The atmosphere was grim, as if the pub didn't want me in it. I'm still aware of it now, a vile feeling. Whenever I go into the ounge to wipe the tables or something, I feel nervous.

We have all kinds of strange things happening here. The gas to the beers is repeatedly turned off. One day, Jack found the gas had been turned off, he went down to the cellar and turned it on then two hours later it had been physically turned off again and no-one had been down there. You will notice that we're without a telephone at the moment. The engineers have been called in several times but they can't find anything wrong. We were without water last weekend. We called in the Water Board, the plumber and everyone we could think of. In the end they discovered that the main stop tap had been turned off which is under Mick's bed. Mick assures us that he hadn't been meddling with it.

One of my daughters was in the toilet late one night after the premises had been closed and she heard groaning in the toilet. She shot out. The ice house is in the far end of the pub and neither of them will go to fetch ice unless someone goes with them.

The gas has been turned on in the kitchen. I came down one morning and thought, 'I can smell gas' and someone had turned it on. We see strange shadows; twice I have seen a large black shape standing behind Jasmine, like a dark shadow.

We used to have a kitchen door that swung both ways. It used to

The Black Star, Stourport, showing the old buildings along the side of the canal.

swing to and fro all by itself, as if someone had walked through it, and each time it would creak and squeak and make such a noise. There would be no draught or wind. It was very eerie. A lady came in one day and said she knew what it was. We had ghosts who wanted the kitchen to be as busy as it used to be, and they wanted the piano moved so that people could bang the keys as they went past. We took this with a pinch of salt but we moved the piano and to our surprise, the squeaking stopped.

We have two ladies visiting us in The Lounge. When we first came I saw them quite regularly, perhaps as much as twice a week, but I haven't seen them lately. The one is very starched, harsh and matronly. I call her Agatha. I know that she's not pleased to see me. She just stands in the corner and stares at me for a few minutes. The other lady, Phyllis, is softer and friendlier. They each come from a different era. I have never seen them together, but Phyllis usually appears a few minutes after Agatha has gone but the time lapse can vary. They're fairly solid but a bit hazy. Mick also saw two ladies there, he described them to me and they're the same as the ones that I saw.

About eighteen months ago I was in The Bar just pottering about, not many people were in there, when I saw a tiny old man sitting on a stool at the end of the bar. The first thing I noticed about him was that his clothes were out of date. He was dressed predominantly in dark brown, with a long coat and a hat similar to the ones that the boatmen used to wear, shaped like a baseball cap but the peak was pushed up. I thought he was quite sweet and I just carried on with my work, so I didn't notice him disappear. I've seen him a couple of times since and one or two customers have seen him as well. We call him 'Bill'.

At this point Mick joins in the conversation:

Only last night I saw a little old man sitting at the bar having a drink. One minute he was there and the next minute he had gone.

About four months ago I felt something touch me. I was standing at the bar, facing the mirror and Martin (another part-time worker) was facing me when something flicked my ear. I turned round but no-one was there. I looked the other way quickly as I thought it might be Beth or Jasmine placing a joke but no-one was there. I said to Martin, 'Who flicked my ear?' He said, 'Nobody'. I got up and looked round as I still thought it might be one of the girls playing a joke but they were nowhere about.

I was serving in the bar one evening with Jasmine. Over the bar is a string of lights and a huge blob of water was hanging from one of the lights. It dropped down on to the counter. Both Jasmine and I saw it drop. Jasmine reached for a cloth. I said to her, 'What are you doing?' and she said, 'I'm getting a cloth to wipe the water up' and I told her, 'There is no water'. It was a huge drop of water but when it fell, there was no water. Jasmine wouldn't go in the Bar afterwards.

Michelle remarks that her husband has seen a white lady. Rather embarrassed, he says:

I'm a disbeliever, but I was just sitting at the bar when I saw a white lady pass across the far end of the bar from the road side to the other wall. She was young and she was wearing a white dress. I thought it might be a wedding dress. She was moving very quickly, I think she would have been running but I couldn't see her legs. I looked round, shocked. Jasmine was sitting at the table, and she said to me, 'Did you see that?'. I thought, 'Well, if she's seen it as well I can't be drunk'. I can't tell you any more about her, it was so quick, I only saw her for a split second.

Jasmine adds:

You should have seen the look on his face. I said, 'See, I told you this place was haunted'. It wasn't a wedding dress she was wearing, it was straight down and it had frills on it.

I often feel uncomfortable, if I go to the toilet late at night I feel that something is following me. Beth sometimes jumps out on me and that makes it worse. Once, I went to go to the toilet at three o'clock in the morning and a man with a beard was sitting on the sofa. I couldn't go to the toilet because I had to go past him to get there. Jack was away but Michelle phoned him to see if he had come home during the night.

I have seen the bearded man twice, the second time Beth and I saw him by my bedroom door. He was oldish with long straggly hair and a long dark beard. He looked 'freaky'. Beth and I looked at each other and back again, and he had gone. We just ran.

We often think someone is waiting to be served but when we come out no-one is there at all. Sometimes, when I'm in the bar I hear a woman's voice talking to me. I can't hear what she's saying, it's just mumbling. Sometimes Beth hears her name called. She comes up and says, 'Yes, did you just call me?'.

The disbeliever, Jack, says that one incident did make him feel peculiar:

We had a big vase of flowers on a table in The Bar. I had bought some flowers for my wife and she had put them in water. I was standing a few yards away by the fire. Suddenly the vase rose up in the air, tipped over, did a somersault and landed on the floor, upright, with-

out spilling a drop. There were no windows or doors open.
A final word comes from Michelle:

Last year, I was standing outside the Black Star when an elderly
gentleman walked past and stopped for a chat. He said, 'Have you
seen the ghost yet?' I asked him, 'What ghost?'. He described the two
ladies in The Lounge just as I had seen them and he knew all about
the little man in The Bar. He said his name was Patrick, not Bill. I don't
know who he was, I haven't seen him before or since.

*In 2002 the tenant and architect of The Black Star were presented with an
award from the Stourport Civic Society for the high quality of the restoration
and innovative use of the combined three buildings.*

An electrifying experience

About ten years ago, the local electrician had an uncanny experience. His
son, Peter, talks about it:

My dad was driving from Kidderminster to Stourport along Wilden Lane,
to do a job for someone.

In the distance, cycling away from him, he saw a chap riding a bike.
Coming from the opposite direction was another car. The cyclist suddenly turned in the road and went through the hedge. My dad stopped
his car and got out and the other car also stopped and the driver got
out. They thought the man had fallen off and had an accident or something and they went to help him. Nobody was anywhere near.

A bit later my dad found out that twelve months previously, a chap
had been knocked of his bike in the same place and at that sort of
time.

The scandal of the abandoned bride

This last story from Stourport goes back to 1914 when poor Ada Mills was
jilted on her wedding day!

Ada Mills was 31 years of age and worked as a servant at Abberley. Also
working there was a young man, Frederica. The Rector had taken Fred under his wing and had paid to have him trained as a chauffeur.

Ada worked for the Rector for three years and during that time Fred and
Ada became 'an item'. Ada began to wear an engagement ring. The Rector's brother in London, Captain Bennett, was in need of a manservant and
so Fred was despatched to the big city but he wrote regularly to his fiancée.
Captain Bennett and his wife were going abroad and everyone thought it
would be a good idea if the two were married, then they could live in the

Captain's flat and look after it while it was empty. Preparations for the wedding were made.

The banns were published in Stourport Church in 1914 and Fred also had them read in London. The wedding was to take place on the Monday and a great wedding breakfast had been arranged. The previous Friday, Fred wrote saying that he would be there.

However, on the Monday, Fred did not turn up. His distraught fiancée wired Captain Bennett to ask where he was. Captain Bennett replied that Fred had gone to Stourport to get married. Fred had disappeared off the face of the earth. Perhaps Ada was pregnant as she later claims to have had Fred's child. Captain Bennett and his wife took her into service and it is on record that they paid for her hospital fees.

Fred was finally found working as a farm labourer in Yorkshire. Ada sued for maintenance for her child but at the Stourport Petty Sessions some curious facts emerged. She was not really Miss Mills, but Mrs Fiuhrer. She had been married about six years previously and had lived with her husband for four months in Cambridgeshire. She said she had not seen her husband for about five years. When she became engaged to Fred, she simply dug out her old engagement ring, blew the dust off it and Fred asked her to wear it for him. All that she got from Fred were packets of sweets.

Ada claimed that her husband had died in a boating accident in 1911 before she started work at Abberley. She said that she had told Fred and both employers about her past life. However, her parents had no idea that she had been married. She had kept her marriage a secret because her father had a hatred of foreigners - and with the 1914-18 war hotting up, Germans were probably top of his most hated list.

The Rector of Abberley and Captain Bennett had looked into the matter and agreed that her husband was definitely deceased. However, the judge said that, as Ada had claimed maintenance under the name of Miss Mills when she was really Mrs Fiuhrer, the case could not go forward and the claim was dismissed.

TITTON - Locals become guerrillas

Although only a hamlet on the A4025 between Crossway Green and Stourport-on-Severn, Titton has a dramatic history. It was devastated by floods in 1879. The Smith family who lived in the Worcester Road woke up to find their bed floating and managed to scramble out of a hole in the roof to safety. The local miller got hold of a boat and rescued his family through a window. Hartlebury Castle is nearby which was garrisoned in the civil wars of 1642-1651. The castle surrendered in 1646 but the parliamentarians regarrisoned it in 1647 when they discovered that the locals were plotting guerrilla action.

For 42 years, Shirley lived in an old house in Titton, going back to1633:

We loved the house and did our best to preserve it. Just down the road was Titton Barracks, where Oliver Cromwell quartered his troops during the Civil War.

Sometimes I had the feeling that there was definitely something in the house. I would feel that I wasn't alone and that someone was watching me.

Twice I thought my husband had come in for lunch, so much so that I stood in the kitchen, talking to him. I thought I saw him standing in the doorway. I was so convinced that he was there that when I looked up to find he was missing, I went to look for him outside. I stood outside the loo door shouting, 'What do you want for lunch?!'. He hadn't even come home from work.

Every now and then we could smell tobacco on the landing. A distant relative came to visit us for the day who always claimed that she was psychic. She said to us, 'Did you know you have a man in brown on your landing? He smokes a pipe'.

My daughter-in-law is an ex-teacher. When we told her that she was selling the house, she said, 'Oh, I'm so glad, because when I was sleeping in your daughter's room a man walked through the wall!' We teased her about it, saying it was just wishful thinking, and she clammed up. She mentioned that he was wearing old-fashioned clothes, perhaps 17th century.

We left in 1998, two families have occupied the house since, I know both of them quite well and neither family have seen or heard anything out of the ordinary.

Shrawley – Highwaymen and a lost castle

The village was once the property of some of the most important people in England. After the 1066 Battle of Hastings, William the Conqueror gave the village to Ralph de Toni, his flag-bearer. Through marriage it descended to the powerful Beauchamps of Holt Castle, then to the Earl of Warwick, the Kingmaker. Written evidence suggested that there was a castle here going back to the 1300s but where was it?

Immediately below Shrawley Court was an overgrown, artificial hillock known as Oliver's Mound'. In 2006, the Shrawley and District Historical Society was awarded a grant of £42,800 by the Heritage Lottery Fund to research the site. To the delight of society members, finds from the site suggested that a castle was here but demolished in the 1300s.

Perhaps Oliver Cromwell built a fort on the castle site and that's how it acquired its name. During the civil wars of 1642-1651 between the royalists and the parliamentarians, Shrawley was held by an ardent Royalist, William Chylde. The parliamentarian Oliver Cromwell bombarded the castle from a field on the other side of the river, still known as Battle Meadow, and there was fierce hand-to-hand fighting. A quantity of human bones was found here in the early 1800s.

The Chairman of the local historical society says that Shrawley was plagued by highwaymen and their ghostly horseman could be one of them:

The village was on the river Severn, near a ford and on the main route from Worcester to Bewdley by road. About three miles away was Redstone ford which lay on one of the main routes to Wales from Worcester. Highwaymen could hide in Shrawley Woods and jump out on coaches and travellers. The road was in constant use until bridges were built at Stourport and Holt in the 1700s, and until larger boats needed deeper waters.

Shrawley is well-known for its ghost rider, said to be a highwayman. The story goes that he galloped through Shrawley Wood one night, failed to see the rocky outcrop and went over the edge.

A few years ago, a young couple were driving from Stourport towards Shrawley when they saw a grey horse galloping along the road towards them. They thought they were going to hit it but, to their amazement, it sailed into the air over the top of them.

Chapter four contains information about Sir George Vernon. He loved Shrawley so much that he arranged to be buried here, in the grounds of his favourite cottage in the wood, away from 'prating priests'.

15. Tenbury Wells and the A433

he mediaeval route between Wales and London ran through Tenbury, as this one of the few places where the river Teme could be crossed. Everywhere in the town are reminders of its ancient past. The three northern arches of the bridge are mediaeval. The old road through the town is still there, now known as Church Street. The old market square still exists. When, in 1248, Henry III gave the town permission to hold a market and a fair, Teme Street was divided into plots for letting to tradesmen and shopkeepers, and the outlines of those plots are still there today.

Stand on the northern side of the bridge and you are in Shropshire, cross to the southern side and you are in Worcestershire.

Hidden treasure and a 'Tump'.

In early medieval times enough people lived here to bring out the early missionaries to preach Christianity. Perhaps Saint Egwin (who founded Evesham) himself came here in the 600s, or Saint Dunstan in the 900s. Both saints were once bishops of Worcester and Egwin particularly made a habit of travelling round and preaching to the larger communities. At first there was probably a plain wooden cross to mark the preaching place, but sometime in about 880 it was replaced by a beautiful carved stone cross. A wooden chapel could have been built over the cross but four or five hundred years later, in late Norman times, a stone church was built with a little tower. The cross was smashed and used as part of the masonry.

The Victorians rebuilt most of the church in about 1865 and to their surprise discovered parts of the old stone cross in the brickwork. It was rescued and is now on display in a glass case in the church, a priceless treasure.

Also in the church, now set in a recess in the wall, is a tiny statue of a cross-legged knight dating back to the late 1200s. This is believed to be a 'heart burial', where the heart was taken out of the corpse and saved. Heart burials were common in the 12th and 13th centuries when it was believed that the heart was the origin of all noble qualities in a man, for example, many of the Crusaders had their hearts buried in Jerusalem.

The remains of the preaching cross.

153

Another reminder of the town's ancient history is the curious hillock in a field 50 yards (about 46 metres) or so south west of the bridge, known locally as 'The Tump'. It could be an ancient burial mound or the base of a Norman keep. Some reckon that it could be where the British hero, Caractacus, made a last stand against the Romans, although places such as the British Camp have better qualifications. Strange to say, although archaeologists have been eyeing this mound with interest over the past few hundred years, it has never been excavated. The 'tump' is now in Herefordshire because of boundary changes.

How Tenbury Wells lost the wells

In the 1700s, bathing and drinking natural waters became very fashionable. When Queen Anne 'took the waters' at Bath in 1702, spas flourished and small towns such as Malvern and Droitwich with natural waters blossomed into large spa towns.

In1839, the local Lord of the Manor, Septimus Godson at Tenbury Court, was not happy with his drinking water and decided to bore a deeper well. Imagine his surprise when he discovered that he was drinking delicious-tasting water with an unusual flavour. The town evidently lay on a bed of natural mineral water. The local vicar sent the water off for testing and discovered that it contained iodine, and therefore had healing properties. Drinking the water was reputed to cure liver diseases, scurvy and glandular swellings while bathing in them relieved gout and rheumatism.

A spa specialist was called in, Dr Granville He had visited spas across England and Germany and written books about them. He recommended that they developed the town into a first class spa with pump rooms, promenades, hotels and lodging houses. The result was that a small red brick bathing house was built next to the Court. It had two baths, one for each sex, and consultation rooms where patients could discuss their ailments with a doctor. After bathing or drinking the water, folk could wander round the grounds of the Court, accompanied by the music of a small band. Dr Granville called in his son, who was an architect, to find a suitable site and design a new town.

The licensee of the Crown Inn next door decided to get in on the act by selling bottled water. However, one well would not be enough to satisfy demand so he bored down on his property until he reached the mineral water at a depth of 42 feet. Godson didn't like the idea of opposition so bought his well from him.

By the 1850's. a manager had been engaged, a Mr Hall, a surgeon from Highgate. Unfortunately, the appointment was a disaster. He failed to bring in the crowds, consequently, not only did the spa become unprofitable but Mr Hall had no income and was penniless. He was constantly asking for money. Even worse, he was accused of stealing. It appears that he removed some Tenbury furniture, presumably from the baths, and placed it in his own accommodation. Mr Hall was dismissed and in 1855, the baths were closed.

In 1861 the railway was coming to Tenbury. The town officials decided that this was the time to restore the baths. The Tenbury Wells Improvement Company thought that the town should attract the working classes, with lodging houses rather than hotels. They found a new site and put out tenders for an architect to design a new bath house. They chose a local architect, James Cranston, who had already designed the renovations for the church at Shelsley Beauchamp and several buildings at Tenbury, including the Round Market, Corn Exchange and National School.

Cranston was inspired by the design of a greenhouse. The new bath house was the first prefabricated building in the county. The wrought iron plates and clips were made in Birmingham and erected on site. A large boarding house and hotel were built next to it and another hotel and a boarding house nearby were extended to take more visitors.

Town officials decided to add 'Wells' to the Tenbury and renamed

The fairy-like bath house.

themselves 'Tenbury Wells'. The change of name was never given approval by the appropriate authorities but in the late 1800s there was a relaxed attitude towards such appendages. For example, the 'Royal' of Royal Enfield, later known for its motor bikes, was never sanctioned.

Unfortunately, the flood of visitors never came. The working classes didn't have the money for such luxuries, the Saturday night soak in a tin bathtub off the wall was as much as they could afford. Also, there were other Worcestershire spas with better facilities such as Malvern and Droitwich. The pump rooms gradually went into decline. They were used for various purposes during the war then in 1945 the building was bought by a brewery. By 1986 the building was in a very poor state and so Leominster District Council purchased it, and restored the exterior to its original condition. Thirteen years later a thorough renovation began with grants from various sources.

As with any innovative building, the pump rooms gave rise to severe problems. The roof was not watertight, part of it sagged and the wrought iron sheets, when regalvanised would not fit the original frames. The renovations are now almost completed.

Cranston may have been inspired by a greenhouse but he created a dainty, fairytale building which is quite unlike any other and is a popular background for wedding photos. The spa may have failed but it has left Tenbury with a building of which it can be proud.

LITTLE HEREFORD

This is border country. Only a narrow strip of Herefordshire divides Tenbury from Wales. Since before recorded history, there were problems between the English and the Welsh. The first King to rule almost the whole of England was Offa, who achieved unprecedented power in 793 by murdering the King of East Anglia who was his guest. There was so much strife on the Welsh border that he built a dyke along the whole of the border, from (what is now) the Irish Sea to the Bristol Channel.

For more than 500 years, the English and the Welsh were at war. In 1055, Hereford was burned down by a Welsh army. William the Conqueror tried to conquer Wales and failed. It was not until Edward I attacked with the largest army then known, of about 1,000 knights and 15,000 foot soldiers, that the land was subdued. In 1402 the English led by Sir Edmund Mortimer fought the Welsh under Owen Glendwr at Pilleth, only about twenty miles away (30 km) from Tenbury over the Welsh border. The English were defeated and thousands of their men were killed. The Welsh camp followers hacked the bodies of the dead to pieces and had to be bribed before they gave them up for burial. Owen Glendwr marched on Worcester in 1405 but failed to fight. It was not until the Act of Union in about 1543 that an uneasy peace was finally reached. Even then both sides of the border were subject to occasional cattle rustling and the spiteful burning of crops.

Horror at the Open Day

Less than three miles (5km) east from Tenbury Wells on the road to Woofferton is a tiny track leading to Little Hereford Church. The tower is thirteenth century and fortified. In the meadow beyond the churchyard the unusual bumps and ridges reveal the remains of a deserted village.

In 1993, the Tenbury Wells and District Civic and Historical Society had done some research on the meadow. Terry Hill was one of the leaders of the exercise:

We were asked by the Worcestershire Archaeological Society to lay on an open day. Three of four of us went from the Society – Howard Miller, John Asquith and myself and we took some ladies whom we intended to train to act as guides on the day. It was a very hot summer evening in August and we were all in our shirt sleeves. The site is little more than a series of platforms. We were walking along these and I was showing them where everything had been, when one of the ladies suddenly clutched my arm so fiercely that her nails bit into my skin and the hairs on her arms stood up on end. She cried, 'Please get me away from this terrible place'. She was in a dreadful state. She said that she could see the roofs of the thatched cottages on fire and women and children being mutilated and butchered. Her husband was in another group so we called him over and he said, 'Oh yes, she's psychic'.

She was so upset that she has since left the Society.

When she described the scene she mentioned two towers, one each side of the site. The following day we scratched about in the soil and we found the remains of a circular tower on the one side. The other side is now under the river but there was a lot of dressed stone in the bank which suggested that a building of some kind was there.

We looked into the history of the site and found that the Welsh raided the area several times. A G Bradley, in his book on *The March and Borderland of Wales* (published in 1905 by Constable) wrote that they had once caught the people before they could get into the church. They put the village to the torch, butchered the children and raped the women. Also, according to Thomas Habington, the Elizabethan historian, the Danes are known to have 'ravenously sacked' this area.

First published in Unquiet Spirits of Worcestershire, 1999.

NEWNHAM BRIDGE – The passenger

The little hamlet, situated where the A443 joins the A456, was once of some importance, as there was a railway station here. An arm of the Severn Valley railway branched off north of Bewdley station and passed through Newnham Bridge. The station was once a busy one, taking local produce to the towns, while from mid-August to the end of September the train was crammed with hop-pickers. Unfortunately it was closed in the Beeching axe of the early 1960s. A garden centre (although this is now up for sale) marks the site of the original station.

From here, the ground climbs steeply and at the top is the Tavern, a Victorian pub, probably built to serve the station. While the engine was being refuelled and watered the driver and his mate would nip up the hill for a couple of pints of home-brewed scrumpy. No doubt they were accompanied by some of the passengers.

A pretty young waitress by the name of Lynette was working at the Tavern in the mid 1990's who says:

Everyone will think I'm crazy when they know what I've seen. I've not a lot to tell, really, it was just one of those things.

One autumn night a few years ago I was working weekends part-time at the Tavern. I had finished serving the lunches and I was washing the glasses in the small sink downstairs in the restaurant area, when I felt the room go so cold that it made me look up and there she

The Tavern at Newnham bridge, with imaginative ghost.

was. She moved across the room and I said, 'Excuse me, can I help you?'. It wasn't until she floated through the wall that I realised what she was. When you walk you bob up and down but she moved across keeping at exactly the same height.

She had on a funny old dress. She was wearing a bonnet, flattish at the back, with a ribbon under the chin. The front bit was peaked up and also the side bit which came over her face, so that I couldn't see what she looked like. Because I couldn't see her face I don't know how old she was but from her figure she couldn't have been that old. She was very slim with a very small waist and a good stature, her back was very straight. The top of her dress went down at the back into a big bow with lots of ribbon, then from the waist it went out and down. The dress stuck out at the front from the waist, not as if she was pregnant but as if she had something inside it, making it stick out. Both of her hands were in this furry muff which she was holding in front of her. The colour was a kind of chocolate brown. Both the muff and dress were the same colour and it was a very nice material with a shine, it looked quite expensive.

She took a route going from the pillar on my left to the kitchen on my right and she must have gone straight through an eight-seater dining table. The pub had not long been redone and the door had been moved about three feet. She went through where the door used to be.

I was so surprised that I pulled a drawer open too far and a glass fell into the sink where it broke.

Lynette's description of the dress is very precise and it would see to belong to the 1830s. When the licensee heard this story, he remarked:

In the 1960s the railway embankment outside the Tavern was levelled out and an extension built. The apparition was seen in this new extension and so, as she was obviously from many years ago, she would have been outside and heading towards the old steps that led down to the station.

First published in Haunted Pubs of Worcestershire, 1998.

ABBERLEY – The time machine

As you drive along the road between Ombersley and Tenbury Wells you can't fail to notice a clock tower high on a hill. This is Abberley Hill, where, in 1405, Henry IV camped with his army, nervously anticipating a great battle. Facing him on Woodbury Hill were the forces of Owain Glendwr, leader of the Welsh. The two sides spent a few days shouting taunts at each other and there were a few light skirmishes. Then the king's army woke up one morning to find their adversary had disappeared. Glendwr's army had crept away in the night.

The clock tower was built by Joseph Jones in 1884. He had bought Abberley Hall fourteen years previously with a fortune made in the Lancashire cotton mills. There are all kinds of rumours as to why he built the clock tower. Some say he did it to spoil the view of a rival neighbour. Others say he did it so that his farm workers would get to work on time. Yet others think it may have been built to give work to the local unemployed. In actual fact, he probably built it as a memorial to his wife.

The hall is now a school. About 30 years ago one of the local teenagers, Sonia, had been baby-minding and it was nearing midnight as she walked back home with her older friend. Invigorated by the cold night air, they decided to call in at the school for some exercise. Then Sonia is certain that she saw a strange sight:

There's supposed to be a grey lady at Abberley, I haven't seen the grey lady but I did see a UFO there. It was about 11.30 at night and I was going into the boy's school to do some PE, local people were allowed to use their gym and it was open 24 hours a day. I was about fifteen and I was being walked home by my friend who was about 26.

The UFO was massive, about fifty feet across, and very close. It was circular and rounded on top and underneath. On the top was a small dome. Underneath were lights all round with a beam coming down from each light.

We both saw it and stood and watched it until it had moved away.

Abberley Hill and the clock tower but without the UFO!

GREAT WITLEY - Scandal at Witley Court

Looking at the ruin which is now Witley Court, it seems unbelievable that only a hundred years ago it was the most luxurious stately home in England.

William the Conqueror gave the manor of Witley to his relative, Urse d'Abitot in 1066, and the manor remained in the hands of the great land-owners until the civil wars of 1642-1651. Then it came into the hands of the Great Industrialists. The first was Lord Foley, the family had acquired their wealth by discovering an efficient method of iron-slitting for nail-making. The family bought the Manor in 1655, improving and enlarging the Jaco-bean house already there. However, they had a problem. They wanted a landscaped garden but in front of the house was the local village, with its conglomeration of thatched hovels. The villages were 'persuaded' to pack their bags and move away to the village of Great Witley so that they didn't spoil the view.

The Foleys built the central part of Witley Court. They also built the beauti-ful Italianate church next year, which came about in a most unusual way. The Duke of Chandos at Edgeware in Middlesex had built himself a large mansion beween 1713 and 1720 but he went bankrupt and had to sell up. The second Lord Foley bought the ceiling paintings by Antonio Belluci and the painted glass of the windows and managed to fit them into his own Church.

Then came a great scandal. The seventh Lord Foley was fat, lazy and a compulsive gambler. The press christened him 'Lord Balloon'. He gambled away the entire Foley fortune so that in 1837, his grandson was forced to sell the estate to the Dudley family.

The Dudley wealth came from coal mines, iron works and limestone quar-ries. Using the Foley house as a core, the house was developed into a splen-did stately home. The costs of the alterations in the late 1850s was £250,000 (worth £10,000,000 today), and this was at a time when a labourer was paid less than £1 a week. The second earl was a friend of the Prince of Wales, later Edward VIII who reigned from 1901-1910. Witley Court became one of the one of the fashionable houses of Europe. Many crowned heads of Europe stayed here.

In 1920, after World War I, the Dudley purse began to run out and the Earl of Dudley's wife died tragically by drowning. The estate was sold to a Kidderminster carpet manufacturer, Sir Herbert Smith. Originally a de-signer, he had worked his way up to become owner and chairman of Carpet Trades. He only lived in a small part of the house and most of the estate was closed. One weekend in 1938 he went away leaving just a skeleton staff and the house caught fire. Only one wing was damaged but World War II was imminent, so Smith decided to auction the estate. A buyer could not be found so the Court was divided into sections and sold to various demolition companies who pulled the house to pieces.

That would have been the end of Witley Court had it not been for an enterprising local group who, in 1967, began a campaign to save the Baroque Church. In 1972 the Department of the Environment undertook the guardianship of the Court and grounds and today the property is in the care of English Heritage. The Poseidon Fountain Restoration Society have managed to restore the great fountain.

Who's that living in my house?

This story came from Lynne, one of the custodians.

When English Heritage took over Witley Court, they first attended to the building itself and made it safe and secure. Then they turned their attention to the drive which not only needed repair but also re-routing. An army of workman arrived to do the work.

Because it was in middle of nowhere, the workmen left their tools and equipment out at night. When they arrived one morning they were upset to find everything had been vandalised.

They approached one of the managers and asked, 'Didn't anyone see them?'. 'Hasn't anybody got any idea who did this?' 'What about the people living in that flat?'

'What flat?' asked the manager.

Between Witley Court and the church is a derelict enclosure with a wall of glass overlooking the site. The workmen pointed to the windows and said, 'The people up there'. The manager explained that it was derelict but they would not believe him. To convince them, she had to get the key, open up, and take them in. The workmen said that without doubt they had seen people up there.

In 2003 English Heritage offered the freehold of Witley Court for £975,000 which was purchased in early 2009 by two ladies.

16. UPTON-UPON-SEVERN AND HANLEY CASTLE

or centuries, Upton-upon-Severn was the only crossing of the river Severn between Worcester and Gloucester. The river could be forded with difficulty at low tide. Until the days of 1400s, travellers were taken across by ferry. Then came unsettled times where it was necessary to get large groups of people across the river urgently, and a bridge was built. A century later, in the time of Queen Elizabeth, the bridge needed to be repaired. A charity was founded to raise money for its repair, and the whole of the county was taxed. By 1593 £700 was raised and two arches were built, however, many people refused to pay the taxes and the work was suspended.

Twelve years later, the bridge had fallen down and the remainder was in a sorry state. Queen Elizabeth had died and James I (the son of Mary Queen of Scots) was on the throne. Parliament, acting under his authority, passed an Act saying that the bridge had to be completed within three years. The finished bridge was a handsome stone structure with five high arches.

Then came the civil wars of 1642-1651 between the Parliamentarians and the Royalists. There was probably more fighting in Worcestershire than in any other county. Armies often destroyed arches after they had passed through in order to delay the enemy. Two arches were blown up in 1643. They were repaired, but blown up again in 1644, repaired and destroyed again in 1651. The story is well-known of the Battle of Upton Bridge. A single plank had been laid across the broken bridge and the royalists were supposed to be guarding it but the tale is told that they sneaked off to enjoy themselves at The White Lion. A group of parliamentarians saw that the bridge was unguarded, managed to get across, were spotted but reached the church where they barricaded themselves in. A posse of parliamentarian cavalry managed to ford the river to rescue their comrades. Consequently, the parliamentarians managed to hold Upton, a valuable strategic position as it enabled them to reach the Royalist camps on the other side of the river.

The bridge brought tragedy in 1832. The cholera epidemic started here, raging through Worcestershire. It began in July but August was one of the worst months when about 30 people died. A special burial ground was opened in a nearby field.

The cholera plaque near the centre of the town.

163

Twenty years later, in the days of Queen Victoria, the bridge was washed away by a violent storm. A new iron one with four spans was built in 1853.

The present cantilever bridge, known as Victoria Bridge, was built in 1940 with a 200 foot span and was considered to be an engineering triumph.

The ghost of Captain Bound

Captain Bound lived 400 years ago but the name can still bring a feeling of terror to those who live in Upton-upon-Severn. Locals will tell you that he was a wicked and cruel man. He married three wives but murdered two of them, one in an upper room of the White Lion. He buried three of them in his cellar. He lived at Soley's Orchard but was greedy for more property so when the old lady who lived at Southend farm died, he held the hand of the corpse and forged her signature on a will in which he inherited the farm. The old lady came back to haunt him and terrified him so much he drowned himself. Another story is that he led a secret life as a highway robber, was finally caught during a highway robbery and hung at the cross roads where the Upton Road joins the Worcester/Tewkesbury Road.

It is said that his ghost was seen so often and frightened so many people that the Rector was asked to lay him to rest. After saying a blessing, the vicar threw a one inch lighted candle into a pool, but the spell was too weak and Captain Bounds was seen again. The local antiquarian, Emily Lawson, in *Recorded Traditions of Upton-upon-Severn* (1880), reports what is said to have happened next:

The ghost 'grew so strong and forward, that he used to ride along the lane on his grey horse in broad daylight. Folk were terrified and put about that they could not bear it any longer and so, three parsons were had to lay him. He'd been very troublesome at Soley's Orchard, and they went to the cellar there, and stood holding hands in a ring, a-laying of the Captain. But one of the ministers – 'twas the rector – had one leg outside the ring, which gave the spirit power. All at once there was a whiz, and something went by and hit him on the cheek, so that the whisker never grew on that side – no, not to his dying day. Still, the three parsons settled the Captain, and laid him so firm in the Red Sea, that we can't be quite sure he's been since, though many say they've heard him'.

The question is, who was Captain Bound and why was everyone so terrified of him? He was born in the early 1600s of a well-established Upton family; his father was a church warden. He was a quiet, studious young man and he himself became a churchwarden in 1640.

His first wife was Mary Cook from a respectable family in Longdon but when they had only been married a year, both she and her two-month old baby died. Then came the first civil war of 1641-1646 when he joined the Parliamentary army and was made Captain. At the end of the war he married again, by a curious coincidence to another Mary from Longdon, this time Mary Higgins. Again, mother and baby died tragically within ten days of each other in the April of the following year. It only took him ten months to find another wife, Margaret Batherne. More tragic deaths followed. She had five children but two of them died in infancy and Margaret died when her youngest child was only three months old.

Despite his sorrows, the captain prospered and bought several fields and houses, including the lease of Southend farm from Mr Bromley.

Perhaps all these tragic deaths gave rise to rumours of murders. Local gossip says that he ill-treated his wives but would he have found a third wife so quickly if he had had the reputation of cruelty? He no doubt treated his tenants and business acquaintances with such severity that his reputation lingers to this day.

He could also be guilty of an act which would have made him very unpopular. When the Parliamentarians were victorious at the end of the war, some priests were removed from their church and consequently their living. The Rector of Upton-upon-Severn, Mr Woodford, had been there many years and was much-loved by his parishioners. He was ejected, and as the Captain was a church warden and a person of some importance he could have been responsible for the decision to get rid of him.

The Captain was buried near the chancel of the church. When a vault was being dug in about 1834, the masons came across his bones and his gravestone. The stone was replaced in the east end of the church, while his skull was made into a drinking cup by a local tradesman who occasionally used it at parties.

Captain Bounds is still said to ride up Rectory Lane on a grey horse, the chain he used for measuring land jingling behind him. There's also a tradition that late on a summer evening in July, the dark figures of the Captain's

A typical gentleman landowner of the 17th/18th century. From an old woodcut.

funeral procession can be seen winding their way along Minge Lane. Emily Lawson, said that she had met a lady who had seen the funeral procession in her childhood. The coffin was covered with a black pall and three or four men were following in black cloaks. The strange thing was, they were going away from the church and not towards it.

The farm at Southend has now been pulled down while at Southey's Orchard, the cellar has been bricked up and the house modernised beyond recognition.

John Dee - Upton's scandalous vicar

John Dee and his signature.

Over the last twenty years or so people seem to have became fascinated by the paranormal. Characters such as John Dee have been researched and re-examined with the result that there has been so much written about him and much of it conflicting that it's difficult to write a straightforward account of his life.

His association with Upton-on-Severn came about because , in 1551, he was presented to Edward VI who gave him 100 crowns. Either he bought the living of Upton parish or he was given it by the king. He could have stayed in Upton for a while but it's doubtful. His home was near the river Thames in Mortlake, London.

He lived during the Renaissance, a time of new thinking and new ideas, but when most people still believed in heaven and hell, witches and magic. Alchemists were hoping to find the elixir vitae, a potion which would give everlasting life, together with the philosopher's stone which could turn base metals into gold.

John Dee was a figure of international importance and Upton-upon-Severn should be proud to be associated with him. He was a mathematician, an astrologer and an alchemist. He was the first person in England to support the view that the world was round and his maps were used by most of the great explorers, Sir Walter Raleigh, Sir Francis Drake and Sebastian Cabot. He trained their crews on how to determine their position by the

stars. He calculated an amendment in the calendar. He was well-travelled, assimilating new ideas and collecting books, consequently at his home in Mortlake, he had the largest personal library in England with over 4,000 books. Even Queen Elizabeth went to see his library. He is thought to have inspired Shakespeare's Prospero in The Tempest and Christopher Marlowe's Dr Faustus.

John Dee was born in London of a Welsh family in about 1527, his father was a wealthy wine-seller. As a child prodigy, he went to University at the age of fifteen. He slept only four hours out of the 24 so that he could spend as much time as possible in study. When he was nineteen he produced a play at Trinity College, Cambridge which was so spectacular that no-one could understand how he managed to achieve such effects. That was when he acquired the reputation of being in league with evil spirits. Some say that he was hounded out of the university.

He travelled across Europe, stopping to research in Flanders, Lorraine and Paris. Queen Mary came to the throne in 1553 and Dee's reputation was such that she used him as her astrologer. Unfortunately he upset the queen, perhaps he gave her an unfavourable horoscope, and he was clapped in prison for several weeks. After Mary's death, Queen Elizabeth employed him as her astrologer. The date of her coronation was based on Dee's predictions.

Money was always a problem. Although many eminent people gave him large sums of money, he was always buying expensive apparatus, chemicals, books etc. leaving his family penniless.

Unfortunately, John Dee is remembered today, not for his great learning, but because of his interest in the occult. His fascination with astrology and

From the top: Astronomy, arithmetic and chemistry (or alchemy).

other fringe sciences led him to investigate the paranormal. By 1582, Dee was about 55 years old and three years into his third marriage when he began to have strange dreams and hear unusual noises in the night. He wondered if the angels were trying to contact him. A year later he met a 28-year old medium, Edward Talbot, later known as Kelly. Some sources say that Kelly was Irish, others that he came from Worcestershire and that he changed his name to hide a criminal past. Dee gave Kelly a crystal ball, and Kelly announced that the angels were sending messages through it. This included angelic language, made up of a series of squares containing letters and numbers and Kelly said that, when completed, it gave perfect truth from God. One of the messages was that they were to swap wives. Dee's wife was not very pleased about that.

In 1584, he and Kelly went to Cracow, probably with all his family, wife and children (between five and eight in number), including his brother. It is said that Count Laski suggested that he could return to Poland with him and work uninterrupted in his castle. Two years later the family moved to Prague. Dee seems to have discovered the secret of electro-plating and was able to coat pieces of metal with silver. He assumed that this was a step towards the discovery of the philosopher's stone and sent a piece back to England to Queen Elizabeth. Finally, their sponsors grew tired of handing over gold but getting nothing in return. Dee quarrelled with Kelly and in 1589 returned with his family to Mortlake, leaving Kelly in Prague.

He came home to find that his house had been ransacked, his precious books had been stolen or burned and his instruments had been smashed. (Others think they were destroyed just before he left home and that was one reason why he left). He turned to Queen Elizabeth for help and eventually, in 1595 she found him a post as Warden of Manchester College. He, who had once consorted with the finest minds in Europe, was now in daily contact with unlearned and illiterate townsfolk.

Unfortunately, in 1605 Manchester was in the grip of the Plague. Dee's wife and several of his children died. Penniless and grief stricken, Dee returned to his old roots in Mortlake, where he died in 1608.

Upton's poison pen writer

In Victorian times, moral codes were strict. Everyone was expected to behave very properly. It even went so far that men were not supposed to used the word 'leg' in mixed company, but to say 'limb' instead. Vicars thundered about the fires of hell from their pulpits.

Imagine the surprise, therefore, of Upton folk when in 1869 they discovered that they had, in their midst, a mystery poison pen writer. The local press received a number of letters of abuse. The object of this defamatory mail was not a person, but the local church building. It was described as ugly and mean. The locals looked at the old church in a new light. Perhaps it was a bit of an eyesore.

Finally, the mystery writer was discovered. It turned out to be the vicar's wife. She wanted a new church, so she was encouraging local people to dislike the old one. Anyway, it worked because in 1878, a brand new church was built with a fine spire and a large interior with plenty of free seating.

Whispers and giggles

Near the centre of Upton-upon-Severn is a sixteenth century house converted into bedsits and popular with students. This is what happened to one of the students, David:

It began not long after we moved in, late in 1987. Doors started opening by themselves - the bathroom door would open as you went town the stairs towards it. Things that I was putting down in my room were being moved. I would put a comb on a chest of drawers and the next minute it would be on the bed. Whenever I went to bed I would feel that someone was watching me. As soon as I started going off to sleep I would sense that something was there.

Then one night I was asleep on my side, facing the wall, when I felt a poke in my back. I had been asleep for some time so it must have

Although most of the old mediaeval church has been pulled down, the tower, with its distinctive cupula, known as the 'pepperpot', has been preserved.

been in the early hours. It was a strong poke, halfway down my back, enough to wake me up. I was very shocked. But the next night I was poked again, and these pokes and pinches not only continued but increased until I was getting very little rest. I didn't see anything, just felt these pinches. After a few weeks I had to move my bed on to the landing so that I could get some sleep.

Another student, Alice, slept in my room one night to see if anything happened to her. Although she was left alone, she woke up in the night to see the shadows of a group of people standing by the chest of drawers.

The disturbances were such a nuisance that the two students asked the the Society for Psychical Research for help. Margaret Webb went to see them and said later that although she couldn't see anything, she could hear a great deal. It sounded like a party. At least eight young girls were in the room and there was much swishing of skirts and female giggling. They evidently wanted to play with this handsome young man and refused to let him sleep. Margaret said that she spoke to them and told them to go back to their own world where there many more handsome young men.

Whatever Margaret did seemed to work and the young man was left alone. Intrigued by this experience, the two students researched the history of the house and discovered that during the last half of the 1800s, the house was used as a girls' reformatory.

First published in Unquiet Spirits of Worcestershire in 1999.

The rattling of dishes

A curious anecdote comes from Mr Raymond who lives near Soley's Orchard.

I had a lodger, a teenager, staying with me. He was the friend of a friend. His parents had moved to Ireland and as he had a job in Upton, he needed somewhere to stay for a few weeks while he gave his notice in and finished the job, so I put him up. He stayed with me for about two months. He was very good and nice to have around, but I did pester him about doing the washing up. I kept saying to him, 'You ought to do some washing up' but he wouldn't do it. I really nagged him about it.

The time came that he was going to leave. I had to take him to the railway station in the morning before I went to work. He needed to get an early train as he had to catch the ferry. Before he went off the day before, I said to him, 'Make sure you come back early and have a good night's sleep'. Sometimes he stayed out with his mates. However, he didn't come back early that evening and I went to bed.

I woke up in the night and I could hear somebody in the kitchen. I thought, 'What's going on?'. I looked at the clock and it was two o'clock in the morning. It sounded as if he was doing the washing up. There was such a noise, the clattering and crashing of the crockery. I thought, 'What's he doing, washing up at this time in the morning?'. It went on for about twenty minutes. It wasn't a dream, my wife heard it as well. I got out of bed but as soon as I reached the bedroom door, the noise stopped so I went back to bed. I assumed it was a protest because I had been nagging him to do the washing up – he'd thought, 'I'll do it and wake them up in the process'.

I got up next morning, went into the kitchen and the washing up hadn't been touched. It was all still stacked. I thought, 'That's odd'. I made him a cup of tea and went into his bedroom and he wasn't there. I looked in the bathroom and he wasn't there either. He had never come back.

I still had to go to work. I left it until the last minute then I had to go. I thought, 'He's left it too late now'. I was just getting into the car when a taxi pulled up. He got out of the taxi and said, 'I'm really sorry, I got stuck at Gloucester'. I said, 'Jump in and I'll take you to the railway station'. Then I told him the story.

He hadn't been back at all and to this day we don't know what the noise was.

HANLEY CASTLE - Hangman's Lane

The castle was on the south side of the village and was built somewhere between 1206 and 1213 by King John. It was the seat of those two great families, the Earls of Gloucester and the Earls of Warwick. Courts were held in the castle and many prisoners were sentenced to death on the gallows. The castle fell into decay at the end of the Middle Ages.

Gallows were of two types, either two poles with a pole across from which hung the noose, or one pole and another protruding from it. This latter type is usually known as a gibbet. Remembering that the death penalty could be imposed for something as simple as stealing a sheep, gibbets were a common sight. In a hanging, the victim was slowly strangled, the idea of standing the victim on a trap door which was suddenly opened is a relatively modern idea. At first, gibbets were placed somewhere near the scene of the crime, but then the hangings began to take place in a designated area such as Newgate and Tyburn. There was a gallows in Worcester in front of the prison. The body was then taken down, and, if it wasn't sent for dissection, it was put in chains and hung on a gibbet to deter others. These later gibbets were usually on a bare hill so that they could be seen for miles around. The aristocracy and political prisoners were not hung but had their heads chopped off instead.

Until 1866, a hanging was a public spectacle. It was a great ceremony, the victim was taken to the gallows in procession, printed 'Confessions' were sold, and the victim usually made a speech before he died. Thousands turned out to watch it.

Alan Thomas has been studying the history of Hangman's Lane in Hanley Castle:

In my school days, in the 1960s, I went to a Boarding School at Rhydd Court School, at Hanley Castle, near Upton-on-Severn. Near the school is the old village green parklands, where in time gone by the old gallows or gibbet was kept for some of the criminals sentenced to be hanged at Hanley Castle court.

Near the village green is a lane named 'Hangman's Lane'. During the daytime this is a quiet and peaceful countryside lane, and the smells from the hedgerows and countryside farms make it a nice place to walk along. But at night time it is a different story. Then it's a very eerie, and in the winter time the fog and mist seem to linger on the ground for a long time. Some of the locals say that if you walk along the lane around midnight, on the twelfth stroke of the clock you might see a man hanging from a tree.

I have been alone in the lane at night and it was very spooky in the dark. I would not like to go around midnight, it would give me the goosebumps!

17. GHOSTS INCOGNITO

or obvious reasons, the locations of the stories in this chapter for a funeral parlour, a hospital, a cinema and a church, all need to be kept secret.

The first story was on one of Ed Doolan's programmes in 2009, in which he held a phone-in for unusual experiences.

I work for a funeral director. A lady came in with her second husband, to arrange a funeral for her first husband. They had both remarried. After the funeral, they took the ashes away but a few weeks later the lady came back to tell me that they couldn't agree where the ashes should be buried and they had had a lot of arguments about it. So I said, bring the ashes back to me, I'll put them in reception and every Friday afternoon you can put a little bunch of flowers with them.

This went on for three-and-a-half years, then one Friday afternoon we had a display on or something, the reception was full and we didn't

Snowdrops cover the floor of this Worcestershire churchyard.

have any room. I said to the lady, 'I'm afraid I can't have the flowers in here next Friday'. She was quite upset, so I said, 'Don't worry, I'll put them in my office'.

I put the ashes on a ledge about two yards (1.8 metres) from my desk. In the afternoon there was such a bang and the ashes came flying across the room and landed at my feet. The Director came running out of his office next door asking, 'What was that noise?'.

After that, they decided to have the ashes buried in Quinton cemetery.

The haunted hospital

A mystery caller gave us this information:
I haven't given my name, I haven't said where the hospital is, either. I have been sworn to secrecy. The manager said to me, 'Have you realised what would happen if this got out? Whatever you do you mustn't tell anybody else'. So I have to be careful not to give anything away.

I have been working there for four years. It's a small hospital, a converted old house, specialising in neurological disorders. Families are sent there with their sons and daughters for respite and it offers overnight accommodation.

Something would happen every couple of months. Perhaps it would go quiet for a few weeks then things would start up again. They could happen at any time. You would do the rounds, lock up and go out and then you would look back at the building and a window would be open or a light would be on when I was certain I had turned them all off before I went. You would go back in the morning and the filing cabinet drawers would be open and papers scattered on the floor when I knew that I left the office tidy. Several times I have heard a scream next door and nobody is there.

Sometimes you could smell burning sugar. There was a story about it. At one time two matrons were there, they were making sweets and one of the children got scalded with burning sugar.

We had people with behavioural difficulties. One of the characters was very difficult and we would let him fall asleep downstairs rather than get him up to bed. He was fast asleep in the lounge and we had gone into the kitchen. We heard a noise and we thought somebody had broken in. The sleeping-in door was propped wide open. We closed it, went out and when we came back it was propped open again. That same night we heard a noise in the front bedroom. It sounded as if a barrel was being rolled across the floor, to and fro across the bedroom.

There was a young lad in there with Downes Syndrome, and when we went up to have a look he was fast asleep. We were all so scared that we wouldn't sleep upstairs but dragged a mattress down and slept on the floor downstairs.

One member of staff saw an old man walk out the wall in the library. We looked through some old press cuttings about the hospital and she recognised him as a member of staff in Victorian times.

On Christmas eve, there was just the boss and me in the hospital. Everything had been prepared ready for a sleepover on Christmas week. At mid-day, the boss went into town and left me to shut the place up. I was in the office when I heard a creaking sound coming from the stairs. I stood at the top of the stairs and shouted, 'Leave me alone!'. The creaks turned into real footsteps. I followed the noise of the footsteps downstairs. As the noise went past the fire doors, each one of them slammed in sequence. The footsteps went into the kitchen and the noise of footsteps stopped but were replaced by a tapping noise that went round all the surfaces in the fitted kitchen. I could hear a noise the other side of the fire door. There was a crack between the door and the floorboards and I could see that there was a movement on the other side.

I had a week's holiday over Christmas and went back in the New Year. The staff told me that they had had restless nights. They couldn't sleep. I told the manager what had happened and he emphasised that I must never tell anyone about it.

The haunted cinema

This is a relatively modern building but the cinema staff have reported a number of strange occurrences. In fact, they find the events on the floor more exciting than those on the screen!
A senior member of staff reports:

A lady and a little girl have often been seen in one or other screens by various staff. A customer sitting in screen 6 turned round and saw a little girl too young to watch the film that was due to start. Thinking she was in the wrong screen she went up to her to help and she vanished. Also in screen 6, the Premier Seats are depressed as if someone has been sitting on them, but no-one has been there. Lots of staff have felt as if they are being followed out of the screens and one of them, Kerry, felt that she was being poked in the back. The staff can sometimes hear footsteps out in the bin room, he public can't get into the area only cinema staff.

One of the security officers, Stuart, having done a screen check, pushed the door to find it wouldn't open. He thought someone was behind the door messing about, he tried to open it again and still it wouldn't open. On the third attempt it opened, he looked round the door and down the corridor to see who was holding the door but found no-one there.

Julie, the duty manager, was washing her hands in the main toilets, when she looked in the mirror she saw a shadow of a lady behind her. She turned round to see who it was but the shadow vanished. On another occasion she was sitting in the office which is situated under the tiered seating in screen 4, when she heard children's footsteps running up and down the stairs in screen 4. She went into the screen to see what was going on to find only adults sitting in the seats.

Gary, the Manager, was asked by a male if he could use the toilets, even though he wasn't going to watch a film. Gary said, 'Yes', but waited for the man to come out. After a few minutes the man hadn't emerged so he sent in security to check if the man was all right. Security found the toilets empty. A few days later he was working one end of the stock rooms when heard Luke, one of the projectionists, talking. He thought this was strange as normally you can't hear people talking from up there, and Luke wasn't due into work until later that day. When Gary saw Luke a few hours later, he said, 'You were in early today'. Luke said, 'I've only just arrived'.

Another projectionist, Paul, was in the projection room on his own before the cinema was open. He was threading the film into the projector when he looked through the window down into Screen 2 to find a man climbing the stairs. Knowing the cinema was closed he ran down into the screen to find no-one.

The Supervisor reports:

I was standing on a podium on a quiet midweek afternoon when out of the corner of my eye, I noticed a young girl run down the corridor into screen 3. I walked into screen 3 after the girl and saw her sitting in Premier Seats next to a woman in a modern dress but no shoes. There wasn't supposed to be any customers in Premier Seats in that screen. When I approached and asked the woman if she had her tickets, so that I could check where she was supposed to be sitting, she couldn't produce any. She hardly spoke. Because it was near the end of the film I told her to stay there this time so she didn't disturb any other customers but next time she should stay in her allocated seat. Then I left the screen, thinking to myself that it was odd that no-one else during earlier screen checks had noticed her up there.

I returned to the ticket stand and about 30 minutes later the film finished and I was expecting to see the woman and little girl come out, and maybe even apologise, but they never came out. There is only one main exit and they did not leave through there. We checked the fire exits and all the other screens but could not find them. They had simply disappeared.

Gill is the Head Usher:

My job is to check that all screens and toilets are clean when I arrive on my shift. I pushed the door to ladies' toilets but it only opened about one foot (approximately 30 centimetres), there was something stopping it so I thought, 'I've hit someone'. I put my head round the door and saw a shadow which vanished. The door then opened.

I was waiting outside Screen One for everyone to leave before putting the lights on to clear up. I spoke to two girls who were just sitting there. By this time even the credits had finished and the music from the cd was playing. They said they would be out in a minute so I waited outside. They did not appear so I went back in again to see what they were doing to find that they had gone.

In the cinema, you walk down a corridor and then you come to the seating. The staff stand at the end of the corridor to make sure that everyone is OK.

Last Saturday, a lady came up to me and said that she had seen something in the one corner. It was a dark shape, it seemed to be about the size of a person and it was just standing there. The lighting was dim and so she couldn't make out exactly what it was. She knew it was not a member of staff because we all were blue shirts except for the two supervisors who wear white. As she was watching it, it disappeared.

A final confession

We only know that this comes from a very old Worcestershire church, parts of which go back nearly 800 years:

My husband was in the choir of our local church for fifty years and I have been in it for a good many years.

Two years ago I was in the church and I was putting the cleaning stuff away after the ten o'clock service so it must have been about eleven o'clock or 11.30. I had locked the gate into the church so that no-one could get in. I put the communal stuff in the cupboard, went back to the altar to put the cloth on and was just checking to see if the candles etcetera were OK when the inside door at the back of the church opened. I had locked the gates but not the door. Someone came up the aisle, up to the altar and knelt down. He was holding a prayer book or a bible, I could see the outline.

He was about sixty, medium height and medium build. Although he was quite clear, it was like looking into the distance, as if there was something in the sky but you didn't know what it was.

Then he turned and went out through the back door and as he went he was more misty.

This has happened to me twice before, about five years ago and about fifteen years ago. Last time I could hear it, there was a faint rustling in the background. The first time it happened was when the vicar had just left to go into the Roman Catholic church.

I was calm about it. I was just on the point of going home when the vicar came round the corner, so it definitely wasn't him.

FOR FURTHER READING

Avery William, *Old Redditch, Being an early history of the town from 1800 to 1850*, republished Hunt End Books 1999
Bridges Tim, *Churches of Worcestershire*, Logaston Press, 2005
Daniels Janet and Freeman Marion, *Pershore Digest*, Dolwilym Publications, 2006
Foxall Alan, *Bentley Manor*, self-published 2009
Hodgson, Carole, various issues of the *Clent Clarion*, Clent History Society
Hurst J D, *Savouring the Past*, The Droitwich Salt Industry, published Hereford & Worcs County Council 1992
Lawson, Emily M, *The Nation in the Parish or Records of Upton upon Severn, 1884*, available on disc at www.upton.uk.net
Newbould Arthur, *Not Just Bricks and Mortar*, self-published 1999, illustrated by Norman Neasom
Palmer Roy, *The Folklore of Worcestershire*, Logaston Press 2005
Park Betty I, *Brinton Park & Sutton Common*, Kidderminster Civic Society and Friends of Brinton Park, 2008
Poultney Bernard & Olive, and Richards Alan, *The Lost World of Hanbury*, Poultney & Richards 2000
Weaver Cora & Osborne Bruce, *Springs, Spouts, Fountains and Holy Wells of the Malvern Hills*, third edition, 2001
Weaver Cora & Osborne Bruce, Aquae Malvernensis, *The Springs and Fountains of the Malvern Hills*, 1994
White Alan, *Worcestershire Salt*, Halfshire Books, 1996

BASIC BIBLIOGRAPHY

Bund Willis JW, *The Civil War of Worcestershire and the the Scotch Invasion*, Alan Sutton 1979

The Worcestershire Village Book, Worcestershire Federation of WI's, 1988
Victorian County History' London University 1913
Pevsner Niklaus, *Worcestershire, The Buildings of England, 1968*, Penguin Books
Florence of Worcester, *Chronicle of Chronicles*, Translation from Latin, available in Worcestershire Record Office
And innumerable other books on the history of Worcestershire.

HELPFUL WEBSITES

www.the spas directory.com for St Werstan
www.adam-matthew-publications.co.uk for John Dee
www.shropshire.gov.uk/extracts for Hanley Castle
www.teme-valley.co.uk/pumprooms.htm for Upton pump rooms
Tenbury History Society website, just google the name.
Wikipedia for Saint Kenelm.

REFERENCES

Braithwaite, J., (2008), Putting Magnetism in its Place: A Critical Examination of the Weak-Intensity Magnetic Field Account for Anomalous Haunt-Type Experiences. Journal of the Society for Psychical Research, Vol. 72.i Number 890 January

Braithwaite, J & Townsend, M., (2006), Good Vibrations: The Case for a Specific Effect of Infrasound in Instances of Anomalous Experience Has Yet to be Empirically Demonstrated. Journal of the Society for Psychical Research, Vol. 70.4 Number 885 October

Budden, A., (1996), The Poltergeist Machine – The Hutchison Effect. Privately published.

Cambrensis, G., (1944), The Itinerary through Wales. J.M. Dent & Sons Ltd

Devereux, P., (2001), Haunted Land. Piatkus

Felton, D., (1999), Haunted Greece and Rome: Ghost Stories from Antiquity. University of Texas Press.

Green, C and McCreery, C., (1975), Apparitions. St. Martins Press

Gurney, E, Myers, F, Podmore, F., (1886), Phantasms of the Living, London

Harte, J., (2001), Personal communication

Houran, J and Lange, R., (2001), 'Ambiguous Stimuli Brought to Life: The Psychological Dynamics of Hantings and Poltergeists' in Hauntings & Poltergeists: Multidisciplinary Perspectives. McFarland & Company

Hufford, D.J., (1982), The Terror That Comes in the Night: An experienced-centered study of supernatural assault traditions. University of Pennsylvania Press.

Lodge, O., (1929), Phantom Walls. Hodder & Stoughton

Persinger, M.A. & Koren, S.A., (2001), 'Predicting the Characteristics of Haunt Phenomena from Geomagnetic Factors and Brain Sensitivity: Evidence from Field and Experimental Studies' in Hauntings & Poltergeists: Multidisciplinary Perspectives. McFarland & Company

Rees, D., (2001), Death and Bereavement: The psychological, religious and cultural influences. London

Roll, W.G, & Nichols, A., (2000), 'Psychological and Electromagnetic Aspects of Haunts' in The Parapsychological Association 43rd Annual Convention : Proceedings of Presented Paper, 364-378

Stevenson, I., (1972), 'Are poltergeists living or are they dead?' Journal of the American Society for Psychical Research, Vol. 66 pg 233-252

Tandy, V, & Lawrence, T.R., (1998), The ghost in the machine. Journal of the Society for Physical Research, Vol. 62, 360-364

Tandy, V. (2000), Something in the Cellar. Journal of the Society for Psychical Research, Vol. 64, 129-140

Thalbourne, M.A., (1982), A Glossary of Terms Used in Parapsychology. London

Thomas, K., (1971), Religion and the Decline of Magic. Wedenfeld & Nicolson.Tyrell, G.N.M., (1973), Apparitions. Society for Psychical Research

Books by Anne Bradford

True Life Ghost Stories
Ghosts, Murders and Scandals I £9.95.
Ghosts, Murders and Scandals II £9.95.
Worcestershire the Haunted County £9.95.
Worcestershire Ghosts and Hauntings £9.95.
The Haunted Midlands £9.95.
Haunted Pubs of Worcestershire £7.50.
Foul Deeds and Suspicious Deaths around Worcestershire £10.99.

Oral History Books
Royal Enfield, the company and the people who made it great £14.95.
Stourport-on-Severn, a history of the town and the area £11.95.
My family and other misfits (an autobiography) £7.00.
Old Redditch being an early history of the town written by
Mr Avery between 1800 and 1850, edited by Anne Bradford £6.95.

Books by John Bradford

Severn's Southern Hills £12.95.
Shropshire's Border Hills £12.95.
The River Teme £14.95.
The River Severn £14.95.